Mark O. Hatfield

The Oklahoma Western Biographies
Richard W. Etulain, General Editor

Also by Richard W. Etulain (*a selective listing*)

AUTHOR
Owen Wister
Ernest Haycox
Re-imagining the Modern American West: A Century of Fiction, History, and Art
Telling Western Stories: From Buffalo Bill to Larry McMurtry
Beyond the Missouri: The Story of the American West
Seeking First the Kingdom: Northwest Nazarene University
Abraham Lincoln and Oregon Country Politics in the Civil War Era
The Life and Legends of Calamity Jane
Calamity Jane: A Reader's Guide
Ernest Haycox and the Western
Thunder in the West: The Life and Legends of Billy the Kid
Billy the Kid: A Reader's Guide
Abraham Lincoln: A Western Legacy

COAUTHOR
Conversations with Wallace Stegner on Western History and Literature
The American West: A Twentieth-Century History
Presidents Who Shaped the American West

EDITOR
Writing Western History: Essays on Major Western Historians
Does the Frontier Experience Make America Exceptional?
César Chávez: A Brief Biography with Documents
New Mexican Lives: Profiles and Historical Stories
Western Lives: A Biographical History of the American West
Lincoln Looks West: From the Mississippi to the Pacific
William S. U'Ren: Oregon Father of the Initiative, Referendum, and Recall

COEDITOR
Basque Americans
Fifty Western Writers: A Bio-bibliographical Guide
A Bibliographical Guide to the Study of Western American Literature
The Twentieth-Century West: Historical Interpretations
The American West in the Twentieth Century: A Bibliography
Researching Western History: Topics in the Twentieth Century
By Grit and Grace: Eleven Women Who Shaped the American West
Portraits of Basques in the New World
With Badges and Bullets: Lawmen and Outlaws in the Old West
The Hollywood West
The American West in 2000: Essays in Honor of Gerald D. Nash
Wild Women of the Old West
Chiefs and Generals

Mark O. Hatfield
Oregon Statesman

Richard W. Etulain

University of Oklahoma Press : Norman

Library of Congress Cataloging-in-Publication Data

Names: Etulain, Richard W., author.

Title: Mark O. Hatfield : Oregon statesman / Richard W. Etulain.

Description: Norman : University of Oklahoma Press, 2021. | Series:
Oklahoma western biographies ; volume 33 | Includes bibliographical
references and index. | Summary: "Focusing on Mark O. Hatfield as
a force in Oregon politics, this brief biography explores the evolution
of this moderate Republican politician from his upbringing to his
election to the Oregon House of Representatives in 1950, then
through his service as an Oregon state senator and as Oregon's
secretary of state, governor for two terms, and United States senator
for five terms"—Provided by publisher.

Identifiers: LCCN 2020058459 | ISBN 978-0-8061-7580-5
(paperback)

Subjects: LCSH: Hatfield, Mark O., 1922–2011. | United States—
Politics and government—1945–1989. | United States–Politics and
government—1989– | Oregon—Politics and government—1951– |
Legislators—United States—Biography. | United States. Congress.
Senate—Biography. | Governors—Oregon–Biography. |
Legislators—Oregon—Biography.

Classification: LCC E840.8.H3 E78 2021 | DDC 328.73/
092 [B]—dc23

LC record available at https://lccn.loc.gov/2020058459

Mark O. Hatfield, Oregon Statesman is Volume 33 in the Oklahoma
Western Biographies.

For the Hatfield family

Contents

Illustrations

Series Editor's Preface

Stories of heroes and heroines have intrigued many generations of listeners and readers. Americans, like people everywhere, have been captivated by the lives of military, political, and religious figures as well as intrepid explorers, pioneers, and rebels. The Oklahoma Western Biographies endeavor to build on this fascination with biography and to link it with two other abiding interests of Americans: the frontier and the American West. Although volumes in the series carry no notes, they are prepared by leading scholars, are soundly researched, and include extended discussions of sources used. Each volume is a lively synthesis based on thorough examination of pertinent primary and secondary sources.

Above all, the Oklahoma Western Biographies aim at two goals: to provide readable life stories of significant westerners and to show how their lives illuminate a notable topic, an influential movement, or a series of important events in the history and cultures of the American West.

This concise biography of Mark Hatfield, Oregon governor from 1959 to 1967, points toward two ends. First, and more important, it provides an overview of Hatfield's very successful eight years as Oregon's chief executive. Second, it places Hatfield in the contexts of Oregon and national politics in the 1950s and 1960s. In his long political career stretching from 1951 to 1997, as Oregon legislator, secretary of state, and governor, and then thirty years in the U.S. Senate, Hatfield never lost an election. He became a leader among western Republicans and then for large sections of the national Republican Party.

In addition to the two extensive chapters on Hatfield's role as governor, this volume provides additional information on Hatfield's formative years as well as a summary of his service in the Senate. This story tries to show why and how Hatfield was so successful as a politician, locally, regionally, and nationally. In Oregon, his never-stop campaigning, his willingness to compromise, and his abilities to communicate his strengths as a leader helped him, as a strong Republican, to win all elections in an increasingly Democratic state.

In his years as governor, and later in the Senate, Hatfield represented a Republican Party that gradually shifted. Influenced by former president Herbert Hoover and the centrist ideas of Dwight D. Eisenhower, Richard Nixon, and Nelson Rockefeller, Hatfield was viewed as a moderate or liberal Republican. By stages, however, his party veered toward the conservatives, from Robert A. Taft and Barry Goldwater and on to Ronald Reagan. Hatfield retained his notable national reputation even as his party moved away from him.

This is primarily a political biography, emphasizing Mark Hatfield's political ideas and actions. But information is also provided on how family, colleagues, and religious influences shaped his political decisions.

Through hindsight one realizes now more clearly the large importance of Mark Hatfield as a state and national political leader. The following pages trace his rise and flowering as a notable politician.

Richard W. Etulain

Preface

I first heard the name Mark Hatfield when I was a senior in college. Had I not been chasing a pretty dairyman's daughter from Tillamook, Oregon, Hatfield would have been my graduation speaker at Northwest Nazarene College (now University) in Nampa, Idaho, May 1959. Instead, I was on the five-year plan, finished the next year, and went off to the University of Oregon for graduate work in English and history.

Hatfield was the Oregon governor in my six years in Eugene. Not only did I get to vote for his reelection as the state's chief executive in 1962, but I was also able to vote for him as U.S. senator in the spring primary of 1966 before completing my doctorate in history and leaving the state ahead of his election to the Senate the next fall.

My attraction to Hatfield followed several paths. I had been raised in a Republican home. I was an evangelical. I already preferred middle-of-the-road politicians, not those who drove decisively to left-wing or right-ring extremes. And Hatfield's energetic youthfulness captured my attention and allegiance. Even after I converted to the Democrats—

my Republican friends said backslid—I found Hatfield to be the kind of politician I wanted to support.

So, this is a sympathetic biography of Mark Hatfield's years as Oregon governor. Even after I make allowance for his mistakes and where I disagree with his conclusions, I think him a role model for politicians.

I wish to clarify the major purposes of the pages that follow. This is, first of all, a *political* biography. I do not emphasize Hatfield's personal life—other biographers need to do that in more extensive and perhaps definitive life stories when more personal information is available. Nor do I place large stress on Hatfield's religious beliefs even though they were the strongest shaping influence on the governor's political life. In that regard, let me point readers interested in the religio-political mixture in Hatfield's career to Lon Fendall's fine book *Stand Alone or Come Home* (2008), where he deals with Hatfield as a "progressive evangelical."

My major emphases are on Hatfield's eight years as Oregon governor, 1959–67. Originally, I had intended to do a thorough book on Hatfield's full career, but finding his largest manuscript collection still closed to researchers I decided to focus on the gubernatorial period. I provide one chapter summarizing Hatfield's earliest years and a second detailing his first experiences in the Oregon legislature and as the state's secretary of state. Then follow two long sections on Hatfield as Oregon's governor. A concluding chapter concisely summarizes Hatfield's thirty years in the Senate and his final years as a professor and in retirement.

This project, then, has been an exercise in remembrance, research, and admiration. I have enjoyed recalling how Hatfield grabbed my attention more than sixty years ago—and held it through the years. Although volumes in this series carry no notes, the appended "Essay on Sources" and extensive bibliography list, and sometimes comment on, the major sources for my research. I wish to thank Lon Fendall and Wes Grandberg-Michaelson for their valuable comments on Hatfield, drawing on their service as his legislative assistants. I am also indebted to Marc Johnson and Walter Nugent for their evaluative readings of my manuscript. Kent Calder and Steven Baker, my editors at the University of Oklahoma Press, have been supportive from the beginning of this project. I am also grateful to John Thomas for his helpful copyediting and to my daughter, Jackie Partch, for the indexing. I have delighted, too, in conversations with my wife Joyce and other longtime Oregonians as we have recalled our days under Mark Hatfield's admirable leadership.

Richard W. Etulain

Mark O. Hatfield

1

The First Years, 1922–1949

In January 1959, Mark O. Hatfield took the oath of office as the newly elected governor of Oregon. After eight years as a state legislator and secretary of state, Hatfield was now stepping into Oregon's highest political office. He would serve eight years, two full terms, and become the state's first two-term governor in the twentieth century. After these years as Oregon's chief executive, Hatfield was elected to the U.S. Senate, where he would remain for five terms, or thirty years. In his forty-six years of officeholding, during which time he never lost an election, Hatfield proved to be the most important political leader from Oregon, in the state and on the national level.

Few would have predicted, judging from Mark Hatfield's early years, that he would become one of the nation's most noted political leaders in the years stretching from the late 1950s to the mid-1990s. His family background and his boyhood and youthful years were not predictive of his later memorable successes.

Hatfield was born 12 July 1922 in Dallas, Oregon. He lived in that small town of 2,700 residents until he was nine, when his parents moved to Salem, the state's capital, just twelve miles east of Dallas. Hatfield grew up in a stable, steady, and religious home. But the differences in background and character of his father and mother introduced valuable complexity to his boyhood and youth.

Hatfield's father, Charles Dolen "C.D." Hatfield, epitomized the tradition and stability of the Hatfield home. Born in April 1872 in Amador County, California, C.D. moved when five with his family to Roseburg, Oregon, where he grew up and attended public schools. Later, he briefly attended Oregon State College in Corvallis, before moving to Dallas. During World War I, he served in the navy. C.D.'s father, a blacksmith, encouraged his son to follow that occupation, which he did as a Southern Pacific Railroad construction blacksmith for forty-two years. In 1919 he married Dovie Odom, and their only child, Mark Odom, was born three years later.

Those who knew C.D. often saluted his diligence and trustworthiness as a husband and father. Biographers Robert Eells and Bartell Nyberg characterized Hatfield's father as a "kind, quiet, gentle man." Another commentator was impressed that, among droves of swearing men at the railroad yards, C.D. avoided foul words. In the political arena, C.D. was a nonassertive Democrat who preferred candidates from that party, although he dissented from Franklin Roosevelt's politics, including the New Deal, thinking that the president wrongly employed the power of the central government to usurp the rights of American citizens. Later, when Mark swung in to support his mother's Republican Party, his father, rather reluctantly, also voted Republican— not because he backed that party but to support his son.

Besides C.D.'s clear record as a diligent worker, he also gained a good name as a devout Christian and churchman. The Hatfield family attended the Methodist church in Dallas, on Sundays and Wednesday nights. C.D. was active in that church as a Sunday school teacher and member of the choir and was recognized for his devotion to Bible reading.

Grandma Birdie Odom's house in Dallas, Oregon. During his boyhood, Mark Hatfield lived a few years in the home of his maternal grandmother. He resided there while his mother Dovie Hatfield went to Oregon State College for her education degree. His father C. D. Hatfield also lived there. Author photo.

C.D.'s role as a parent greatly expanded when his wife Dovie decided to commute to and stay in Corvallis during the week to attend Oregon State College and obtain her teaching credential. Renting out the family home in her absence, C.D. and Mark moved in with Mark's grandmother—Dovie's mother, Mary Alice "Birdie" Odom—where grandma served as a warm, supportive surrogate mother. Meanwhile, C.D. remained at home during the evenings and forged a strong link with his young son.

In his autobiographical memoir *Against the Grain* (2001), Hatfield explained several facets of his father's character. When C.D. became nearly the sole parent in Dovie's absence, Hatfield recalled, "I knew the stability, the confidence, the security of his strong presence." At home in the evenings, father and son listened to radio programs, read together, looked at maps, and relished "the wonders of geography."

On more than a few occasions, the two Hatfields, father and son, took trips. They fished Oregon streams, visited family members adjacent to the Grand Ronde Reservation, and took refreshing hikes in the woods and along the coast. In these ways, early on, Hatfield felt comfortable with his dad—warmed by the companionship and dependability of his father.

Hatfield also saw aspects of his dad's personality that other observers missed. Mark repeatedly pointed to his mother's and grandmother Birdie's independent streaks, but in viewing his father's decision not to return to farm with his family, as requested, and deciding to pursue another path, C.D. too "was exactly like Mother in that way; he tried his own path, though perhaps more quietly."

That independent streak in C.D. impressed his son throughout his life. In fact, his father's sturdy stances provided a major pillar for Hatfield's own life. As governor and senator—indeed during his entire political career— Mark followed his father's advice: "Dad taught me never to be afraid to stand alone, and so I stood." On several major national issues, Hatfield stood alone—or nearly so—following his father's valuable admonition.

C.D. additionally helped shape his son's social conscience. That molding occurred, Hatfield remembered, when his family, especially his father, dealt with needy people in hard times. If hoboes knocked at the door or appeared in the backyard, Hatfield's father would leave unchopped wood for them to earn a meal. If that was impossible, the Hatfields provided food and on some occasions invited the wanderers into the home to share a meal at the family table. In these happenings, young Mark saw firsthand the difficulties some homeless folks had in finding sufficient food. Recollecting, Hatfield noted the impact of these happenings on his outlook: "This was the beginning of my lifelong lessons in inclusiveness, pluralism, and aiding the less fortunate—three virtues well practiced in my home."

Hatfield's remembrances of his mother were equally positive, and perhaps even more encompassing. If C.D. became a model for wholesome, encouraging father-son relations and diligence and stability, his mother represented educated ambition, energetic drive, and upward mobility for her son.

Dovie Odom Hatfield obviously aspired to rise above her own modest, challenging beginnings. Born in 1893 in Morristown, Tennessee, a Republican, pro-North part of the South, Dovie, the oldest of five children, moved with her parents and siblings to Oregon in 1903. Tragedy struck the family when husband and father Thomas Austin Odom was killed in a wagon accident in 1912. Dovie's mother Birdie became a widow at age thirty-seven, with no financial support in view. At age nineteen Dovie became the chief help to her nearly penniless mother, and together they opened the family home to boarders—and survived although in straitened circumstances. These demanding family responsibilities quickly matured Dovie and seemed to motivate her to seek an education to escape the tight times of her mother. In two years of schooling at what became Western Oregon University in Monmouth, Dovie earned a teaching certificate in 1916 and began teaching in back-country Oregon before returning to Dallas to teach in her hometown. In 1919 she and C.D. married, and son Mark came along in 1922, but Dovie did not give up on gaining an even better education. As her obituary put it many years later, Dovie was "determined to get a college education despite the start of the Depression in 1929."

After the two earlier years at Western Oregon and two additional years at Oregon State College (1928–30), Dovie returned to teach in Dallas, then pushed hard for the family to move to Salem, which they did in 1931. Dovie taught home economics at Leslie Junior High School (the same junior high Mark attended) in Salem for thirteen years before retiring in 1944. After leaving the classroom, Dovie worked for a brief period in the Oregon Department of Revenue.

Along with her own education, Dovie pushed for a good education for son Mark. She seemed driven to step well beyond her own origins. The challenges soon doubled. Not only did her own family background contain little in the way of education, but now her husband, although always exhibiting perseverance and stability, did little to encourage schooling for his son. Mom would become the educator and, as one commentator put it, Dovie was "wrapped up in Mark."

Mom's influences also proved paramount in the areas of politics and religion. Although C.D. and Dovie brought differing Democratic and Republican perspectives to the dinner table, their exchanges were rarely heated. Still, Mom won out. Even before Mark became a teenager he was participating in Republican rallies, handing out brochures and other political propaganda.

Dovie also won out in religious matters. While in Dallas, the Hatfields attended C.D.'s Methodist church, but when they moved to Salem they became Baptists, the denomination of Dovie's choice. For the most part, Mark identified as a Baptist for the remainder of his life. What Dovie had introduced early on to her son, as far as religious affiliation was concerned, had a lifetime impact.

Hatfield's comments reinforced these supportive comments about his mother, but he also advanced other opinions with unusual twists. For Hatfield, his mother was a "feminist," even before that word was in wide circulation. As he succinctly put it, "Mother was so independent she had no use for tradition for tradition's sake." She wanted no usual church wedding—surprising for a devoted church woman—and talked C.D. into eloping. Sometimes, as Mark suggests, not everything flowed smoothly after Dovie's untraditional decisions. Another terse comment from son Mark reveals his moderate ambivalence about some of his mother's actions. "Mother was as wonderful as a mother could be," Hatfield began, then added, "but it's true she didn't exactly settle down to motherhood like all of my schoolmates' mothers had."

Grandma Birdie Odom was the third of the triumvirate who did so much to shape Hatfield's earliest years. She filled in for the years as a mother when Dovie was off to school. Maternal, a survivor, and committed to family, Grandma served as a second mother while Dovie was pursuing further education. Essentially without education, burdened with the heavy loss of her husband, and now a widow in challenging economic circumstances, Birdie Odom nonetheless found time to provide much-needed support to C.D. and his son in a time of need.

Hatfield's first years were spent in Dallas, Oregon, where he lived for nearly a decade. Looking back seventy to seventy-five years later, he had strong, warm memories of his early life in Dallas. His recollections were nearly always uplifting, recalling the spirit of community, friendship, and small-town camaraderie much more than tensions, conflicts, or economic hardships. As Hatfield remembered skipping down Main Street and recalled sauntering into grocery, drug, and clothing stores, he recollected friendly contacts with merchants, neighbors, friends, and other townspeople.

Hatfield's mental map of life as a preschooler and grade school boy suggests a good deal about the outlook of a youthful Mark Hatfield—as well as about the tenor of his memories recalling his boyhood days. He viewed Dallas a wholesome and holistic community, its life orchestrated primarily by the timber industry with tight links to lumbering and the daily routines of work at the saw mill. The work and sounds at the mill were as marching and sustaining orders for the many workers and their families in the town.

This optimistic view of the timber industry and lumbering generally casts light on Hatfield's later political support for the industry, which his environmentally motivated critics always thought far too strong.

Not surprisingly, Hatfield's memories of Dallas included a good deal about religion and politics, although sometimes one wonders if he weren't reading his life backward rather than forward in these recollections. Still, these were the two most important arenas of activity for most of Hatfield's life. The weekly services and sermons at the Methodist church included the Hatfield family, and the parents enjoyed dressing up their son for these occasions, even making him look, some thought, like a "dandy." Even in these preteen years, Hatfield realized his mother was less strict and less a fundamentalist than many other evangelicals. For Dovie, attending movies, participating in dances, and, later, indulging in smoking and drinking were not unforgiveable sins. From his Dallas to Salem years, Hatfield was not much of a questioner of his religious faith. As his biographers Eells and Nyberg write, "Rebellion was not an ingredient of the boy's personality; he gave no sign of questioning" the Methodist or Baptist "perspective."

Before he became a teenager, Hatfield energetically participated in political activities. At age ten in the election of 1932, Mark pulled his wagon filled with political information supporting Herbert Hoover into several neighborhoods. Later he would become an enthusiastic Hoover fan, but at this early stage he probably acted more out of his mother's encouragement than from his own political drive. The Hatfields were already opponents of Franklin D. Roosevelt before they moved to Salem, with husband C.D. agreeing with his Republican wife in their criticism of the rising Democrat. And Grandma Birdie Odom was always an outspoken opponent of the New Deal president. Yet Hatfield heard his father grumble when his wife and mother-in-law supported a woman running for office against a male candidate. For C.D., a woman's place was at home, not out in politics.

Surprisingly, Hatfield was convinced that "cultural sophistication was top notch in Dallas." As symbols of the small town's cultural achievements, he pointed to the band concerts the family attended, their enjoyment in listening to traveling singers, and the attraction of visiting the theater for silent movies. For the youngster—and for the senior citizen looking back—Dallas, Oregon, was no social or cultural backwater.

Indeed, Hatfield was convinced that his first years in Dallas taught him several valuable lessons for later life, particularly in his political worlds. It was a sense of community that resonated most when Hatfield recalled his beginning years in Dallas. Doors were open and left unlocked, neighbors helped one another, and the town looked after its sociocultural needs. Thinking about this warm, comforting town spirit when writing at the end of the twentieth century, Hatfield opined that the United States had lost these binding links, especially in cities. "We've forgotten how to be with each other and truly listen, even when we disagree." He continued: "Instead we have created more and more walls that divide us."

Finally, Hatfield was convinced, too, that the time in Dallas taught him important lessons about human-land relationships, connections he remembered for a lifetime. In fact, Mark was euphoric about fishing holes, hikes in the woods, vacations in numerous Oregon landscapes, and the everywhere wildlife. "Our mountains, ocean, waters, deserts, gorges, and forests"—they were unforgettable and continually nourished him.

The Hatfield family's move to Salem, which Dovie Hatfield energetically pushed for, took place in 1931. The move proved to be a key to Mark Hatfield's future. In the state capital city, he was now located near the state legislature and governor's office—places where he eventually would reside and lead. Before he won election to those offices, however, the young Hatfield was furthering his schooling, learning political lessons, and making important, new connections.

Not all facets of the transition to Salem went smoothly. The switches to a new, more urban school for Mark, a new job for Dovie, and a change of work location for C.D. were challenging. But the largest difficulty came in trying to find a home that fit the family needs. Before they were able to find that house, the Hatfields rented and moved out of four different rentals. These moves took them in and out of town in the first years in Salem.

Hatfield finished his pre-college education in Salem. After completing grade school and Leslie Junior High (in 1937), he enrolled in Salem High School (now North Salem High School), which he attended from 1937 through 1940. Interestingly, even though Hatfield provided a few bits and pieces, especially about political and religious experiences, he did not write extensively about his teen years. Perhaps this was, he wrote, because his adolescence was "pretty standard."

Most of what Hatfield stated about this time years later dealt with his growing interest in politics. The major lesson he thought he learned during his teens was the importance of political participation. Speaking later to this point in his classes, Hatfield urged students to jump into political organizations, take part in campaigns, volunteer for political activities, and read about politics. Hatfield did all these as a high school political apprentice.

Specific political happenings snared Hatfield. When U.S. Postmaster General James Farley came to Salem to dedicate a new post office, Hatfield played his clarinet in the high school band at the dedication. He remembered well how Farley had thanked the rain-drenched audience and band for their attendance and later even sent a letter of appreciation to band members for their participation. In the elections of 1932 and 1936, Hatfield supported Herbert Hoover and Alf Landon as unsuccessful candidates against Franklin Roosevelt. So convinced was young Mark that Landon would defeat the incumbent Roosevelt that he bet seven milkshakes on Landon's win. As the campaign heated up, Hatfield bet more milkshakes—so many that it took several months to pay back the costs. But the young political aspirant learned a lesson: do not bet on politics.

Never a successful participant in organized athletics, Hatfield turned to politics as his chief sport. Parades and campaigns captivated him. Anything dealing with his hero Hoover also kept him intrigued. Drawn to Hoover and other Republicans rather than to Roosevelt and the Democrats, Hatfield became a "rigid isolationist" as a teen and came to understand the sometimes "minority role" of politics when the Democrats remained in the White House from 1933 to 1953.

In Salem, Mark and his family joined the Baptist church when he was thirteen. As he became an older teen, he faced the complicated Baptist (and general evangelical) reactions to "sinning." Lon Fendall, Hatfield's close friend and staffer, notes that the Baptists "held to something like a two-tier system of 'forbidden behaviors.'" The more negative "sins" were sexual misbehavior, drinking, and smoking. Less repugnant were dancing, movie attendance, card playing, and gambling. Dovie Hatfield was less legalistic about the latter activities, so that, as an older student, Hatfield smoked and drank moderately without eliciting parental criticism. He even enjoyed blowing tobacco smells into his clothes to upset more fundamentalist churchgoers.

More difficult for Hatfield was the increasing sterility of his religious journey. He found that by the time he began college in 1940 his beliefs had become matter-of-fact, sometimes lifeless, and lacking vibrancy and meaning. It was as if his "Christianity was rote, with no particular relevance to my everyday life." After his college years, a stint in the U.S. Navy, and graduate school at Stanford, the tenor of his faith would change while teaching at Willamette University and under the influence of some of his students.

Looking back on his public school days, Hatfield saw lessons he learned during his teen years. One was his growing addiction to reading. "I fed my interest in books," he wrote in his first book, *Not Quite So Simple* (1968). Teachers, seeing his interest especially in politics, encouraged his wide reading. Early on, Mark Hatfield became a bibliomaniac.

Hatfield credited his book learning as a giant aid in helping him to adapt to change and to conflicting points of view. His reading aided him in adjusting to dramatic events like the Depression, World War II, and the Roosevelt presidency. Over time, Hatfield became a book collector. On his special list were books about Hoover, Abraham Lincoln, and other presidential biographies.

Notably, Hatfield chose not to treat in *Against the Grain* and his other books a tragic event that occurred just as he finished high school. On 10 June 1940, Hatfield, then seventeen and two weeks past graduation, was driving north to Salem in his mother's Chrysler when the car struck and killed pre-teen Alice Marie Lane. In court, Hatfield testified that he had not seen the young girl when she darted across the rural road. He was not criminally charged for the girl's death, but later in a civil suit the Lane family won a settlement from the Hatfields. In 1943 the Oregon Supreme Court upheld the civil court's decision. Hatfield never wrote of the traumatic event, but, as we shall see, Senator Wayne Morse used the tragic happening, unsuccessfully, to denigrate Hatfield's honesty on the eve of his gubernatorial election in 1958.

Hatfield spoke of a handful of other school experiences that impacted his later years. For the first time in his life, for example, he met nonwhite students, leading him to think about inclusion. His interests in books drove him to learn, to enjoy examining history and politics. He even tried his hand at school politics, running unsuccessfully for senior class president, losing to his cousin Elvin Holman.

Hatfield's decision to enroll in fall 1943 at Willamette University in Salem made increasing sense. Willamette was small, about eight hundred students, a Methodist college for a young man of Methodist heritage, and close at hand. The university also had a history of students involved in politics (especially since it was located in the state's capital) and had produced several Oregon politicians. And, of course, Hatfield could major in political science, which he soon decided to do.

In fact, Hatfield betrayed his addiction to politics in the months leading from his high school to his college years. In the presidential election of 1940, as he had done in 1932 and 1936, Hatfield revealed his ties to the Republicans in a series of illuminative marches, programs, and peppy meetings celebrating the nomination of Wendell Willkie in his run against Democratic incumbent Franklin Roosevelt. Hatfield was even more attracted to Willkie when the Republican candidate chose as his running mate Charles McNary, a popular Oregon politician and one of the state's U.S. senators since 1917. Later, Hatfield confessed, too, that Willkie's support of internationalism in foreign affairs helped bring him out of his isolationism.

Hatfield also nourished his political fantasies during the summer months and into the fall of his freshman year at Willamette. Working as a capitol guide, he led visitors through the capitol building, showing the tourists the legislative and judicial areas. He particularly enjoyed opening up the governor's office during the weekends. When alone and with a key to the gubernatorial quarters, Hatfield sometimes hopped into the governor's chair, leaned back, and

Hatfield at Willamette University in Salem. From 1940 to 1943, Hatfield attended Willamette University, completing his BA in three years. An honor student, he was also a campus leader, participated in campus politics, led fraternities, and directed student activities. *Wallula* (Willamette University annual), 1944. Courtesy Willamette University Archives and Special Collections.

put his feet on the executive's desk. As he recalled later, these were moments of fantasy, which became real nearly twenty years later.

The university's campus newspaper, the *Willamette Collegian,* and its student annual, the *Wallula,* document Hatfield's rise from a relatively unknown freshman to a highly recognized graduating senior in his three years at the university. The two outlets disclose how active Hatfield became in political, fraternal, and other student areas. He was beginning to show his true colors as an ambitious and talented leader.

The surge in campus politics came first—and extensively. By the opening of Hatfield's second year at Willamette, he had been named president of the Republican Club. In December 1941, just as Pearl Harbor jolted America, Hatfield was named acting mayor when he took over the city on DeMolay Day, a time set aside to honor the organization that sponsored and encouraged young men. Hatfield continued to be active in the Republican Club throughout his college days.

Early on, Hatfield likewise joined the Kappa Gamma Rho, one of the most active fraternities at Willamette. His emergence as a political leader on campus repeated itself among his fraternity brothers. By January 1942 he was secretary of the KGR and by the following May vice president. When the campus newspaper looked for a spokesman who could describe the enthusiasm that accompanied African American singer Paul Robeson's presentations at Willamette, sponsored in part by the KGR, they turned to Hatfield for the moving details. Later Hatfield was named to a committee to provide planning goals for fraternities.

Even more unusual was Hatfield's selection to serve as chairman of the Friday student chapels. It was a new student position on campus, having been previously directed from the university president's office. This charge meant that Hatfield was now serving in one of the most important student leadership positions. His role as student chapel leader captured more than a few lines in the campus newspaper. In addition, Hatfield led the annual May Weekend visitations to campus. It was a time-consuming assignment, calling for many hours of planning.

The number of offices to which Hatfield was elected or selected is nothing less than amazing. In addition to his elected leadership roles in campus politics and fraternity organization, he was also elected a class officer and selected as a member of the Blue Key, the honorary fraternity for juniors and seniors with high marks in scholarship and student leadership.

Beyond these roles to which he was elected or selected, Hatfield joined several other groups or served as their campus representative. A member of the newly revitalized International Club, he participated in library, musical, and dramatic organizations and was the Willamette contact for Salem's Community Concert group.

Despite all these activities and his heavy class load year-round for three years, Hatfield did well in his courses. His selection for the Blue Key honors club not only signaled his track record as a campus leader but also indicated his high marks in his classes. Hatfield majored in political science and history, taking several courses from Robert Moulton Gatke, an expert on the history of the Pacific Northwest, the Willamette Valley, and Willamette University, and who taught more than a half century at the university. Hatfield chose courses in the social sciences and humanities, with less emphases on the sciences and mathematics.

Pushing hard to complete his college in three school years and three summers, Hatfield experienced both a major disappointment and a notable success in his final college months. In the 9 April 1943 issue of the *Willamette Collegian,* the newspaper announced Hatfield's candidacy for student body president. The announcement trumpeted Hatfield's leadership roles in campus activities such as May Weekend, fraternity gatherings, and student chapel direction. The write-up also included Hatfield's campaign promise "to make sure Willamette's student body government functions during the summer session." Hatfield and his major competitor, John Macy, expected to enroll in summer courses.

The next issue of the campus newspaper, 16 April, carried the disappointing story of Hatfield's loss in the run for ASWU president. John Macy had gained 169 votes, 53 more than Hatfield. In turn, Hatfield had run ahead of Hollis Huston, a third candidate in the election. Macy, a member of the Alpha Psi Delta fraternity, had a "long record of student activities," was a track "stand out," and served as junior class president at the time of the election. In his much later memoir, *Against the Grain,* Hatfield spoke of the student body election as one of his only two losses and saluted Macy as a "very well qualified" student leader.

Much more uplifting was Hatfield's unqualified success as the campus commander in a push for World War II bonds. For several weeks from late summer into early fall of 1943, Hatfield was engaged in an important campus war effort. In mid-July in one of his few letters to the editor, Hatfield urged Willamette students to launch a Victory Drive to support the war effort. A week later in an article titled "Hatfield's the Man," a *Collegian* reporter fingered Hatfield as *the* person to head up the drive. "His ability as a manager and leader," particularly in his work with student chapels, his acquaintance with possible townspeople contributors, and his direction of the May Weekend festivals, proved that he should lead the war drive.

The selection of Hatfield as chairman of the Victory Drive came in August. The graduating senior was pleased with the appointment. He would "strive to make the campaign a success and promote it, so that it can be carried on throughout the school year as a permanent organization." Launched in the first week of September, the bond drive exploded well beyond its original goal of $5,000. By the first of October, contributions from the campus and community totaled more than $26,000 for the purchase of war bonds and stamps. Hatfield, noting the success of the drive, thanked faculty and students for achieving the great success with the Victory Drive. Having finished his undergraduate work at the end of summer session, Hatfield was not on campus during the final days of the drive. In fact, in October, in a first fall commencement exercise, Hatfield and eight other students received their diplomas after completing their bachelor of arts program the previous August.

Hatfield and his family had made a key decision at the end of the 1941 school year that shaped the remainder of his time at Willamette and in the years immediately following in the U.S. Navy. The explosive news of the Japanese attack on Hawaii's Pearl Harbor on 7 December 1941 was a game-changer for Hatfield. Beforehand he and his parents were confirmed isolationists, opposing President Roosevelt's efforts to aid the European allies in their fight with Axis nations. But as Hatfield put it later, "In a shocking flash, Pearl Harbor changed all that." Hatfield told his parents he "would be going to war." Like his father before him, Hatfield chose the navy and immediately looked for ways to get into the service quickly. Realizing the desires of Hatfield and dozens of other young men and women, the Willamette administration encouraged the students to join the naval reserve, and the university put into operation the compact academic program that allowed a college degree in three years. Within days after his graduation, Hatfield was on active duty with the navy.

Hatfield was afraid the navy would not accept him into its ranks. At nearly six feet, Mark tipped the scales at only 130 pounds. Would the reserves take a "scrawny" candidate like this? An unnecessary worry because the navy needed thousands more to man their sea domains.

For quick, almost overnight training, Hatfield traveled to New York and then to California. In the cold environs of Lake Champlain in upstate New York, he gradually realized the upsetting truth: he was preparing for war. More than a few of the two thousand servicemen, once they too sensed what lay before them, expressed their desire for office or other noncombative roles.

These few weeks of training took Hatfield to new areas of the country. While in the Northeast, he visited New York City. The press of large crowds were amazing; so were the numerous huge buildings. On one train trip he chanced to meet first lady Eleanor Roosevelt. After introducing himself, Hatfield and Mrs. Roosevelt carried on a brief conversation. Ever after, Hatfield recalled how much the president's wife impressed him with her openness and willingness to listen to his story.

A few weeks later, Hatfield was in San Diego to complete his final training before going into active duty. He was surprised to learn he would serve as a "wave commander," moving marines and their gear in small boats from their troop ships to beaches of combat. Then on to Hawaii for the last few days of simulated "wave work." Where they would head into battles was a top secret, although Hawaiian cab drivers told them they were certainly headed to Iwo Jima.

Eighteen months after completing college and shortly after finishing his hurry-up naval training, Hatfield and nearly four hundred sailors and officers were aboard the USS *Whiteside* approaching the shores of Iwo Jima, on 18 February 1945. The next day the invasion and vicious battle of Iwo Jima began; it lasted until 26 March. Some of the fiercest fighting of World War II took place on this small volcanic island located 750 miles southeast of Japan. Of the 21,000 Japanese soldiers on the island, 19,000 died in battle, and Americans suffered 26,000 casualties, with 6,800 dead.

Hatfield never forgot his traumatic experiences at Iwo Jima. Danger and death faced him and his men as they shuttled marines onto shore, and then, even worse, had to carry the wounded and dying back to the *Whiteside*. The Japanese, in a suicidal attempt to hold on to the island, fired on the beach-bound boats and maintained an incessant threat to Hatfield and his fellows and their "wave work." As the violent days wore on, Hatfield stumbled ashore to find dead bodies littering the beachhead and just beyond. The horrors of war were at hand. Just before Hatfield left the ravaged island, he witnessed—from a distance—the famous raising of the flag over Iwo Jima that became an iconic symbol of American victory in the Pacific.

Then on to Okinawa, where equally violent warfare took place between April and June 1945. On this southernmost of the five islands of Japan, Hatfield experienced horrendous warfare, with 95,000 Japanese dead and 12,000 Americans dead or missing in a series of murderous battles. At Okinawa the attacks were not from guns in elevated areas but from kamikaze planes and swimmers daily threatening ships and sailors.

These horrific war experiences led Hatfield to adopt "a fatalistic attitude." If an enemy bullet had his name on it, so be it. Nothing could be done to avoid such a violent death. But, as Hatfield admitted, when he and his comrades accepted this "empty bravura," they were simply advancing a stiff-upper-lip philosophy to strengthen themselves and others.

Leaving Okinawa, Hatfield's convoy sailed to the Philippines to plan for an invasion of Japan. While there, they heard of the bombing of Hiroshima (6 August) and Nagasaki (9 August). One month after the atomic bomb dropped on Hiroshima, killing between 90,000 and 146,000, Hatfield and a few other servicemen visited the decimated city. It was a scene of endless horrors, with most of those killed from civilian families. The Japanese held back from Hatfield and his fellows until the Americans began to share their lunches with the obviously hungry Japanese children. Although Hatfield and the others had been taught to hate the Japanese as evil killers, a spur-of-the-moment act by Hatfield changed everything. He picked up a Japanese child and almost immediately "was purged, spiritually renewed as hate flowed from my system." No longer were the Japanese enemies but fellow humans—and now in dire need. Hatfield's "hatred had gushed out, transmuted into the powerful balm of compassion."

But Hatfield's soul had been scarred by what he saw in those indescribable hours at Hiroshima. He never forgot the destruction of human life and civilization he saw there in the virtually destroyed city. If one tries to understand Hatfield's subsequent opposition to most wars, particularly to atomic and nuclear warfare, the seeds of opposition were sown in the ravaged landscapes of what he saw and felt at Hiroshima. Hatfield wrote of the experience: "The sights of war haunted me"—and he might have added that thoughts about war haunted him for the rest of his life.

Before Hatfield and his group returned stateside, they traveled on to Indochina to pick up a contingent of Chiang Kai-shek's troops to return them to China to fight the communists. While in Haiphong, Hatfield wrote to his parents describing the poverty and squalor he saw the Indochinese suffer under the lion's paw of French domination. Hunger and filth covered the people and the land. Here again attitudes sprang up that would shape Hatfield's subsequent political positions. He later courageously opposed the Vietnam War, viewing American participation in that Southeast Asian country as negative and ill conceived as the earlier French domination.

In 1946, after a brief assignment on shore patrol in the Bay Area, Hatfield returned to Oregon. His war experiences were opinion making and emotion shaping. Later, he could not watch war movies without his eyes filling with tears. And, for the most part, he opposed war making from then on.

What would Hatfield do next? He had not decided on his postwar plans while he was still in the service. What he most wanted was to return home. Then he would decide the future.

His initial decision at home led to failure—perhaps the most disappointing happening Hatfield experienced in his career. In fall 1946 he decided to enroll in law school at Willamette. It took but a few months for Hatfield to realize that he had made a wrong decision: law school was not for him. He was never expansive about why he disliked law school, although he did claim, with more than a bit of leg pulling, that he had dropped out before he was flunked out. Perhaps Hatfield now realized that teaching politics at the college level or running for public office both interested him much more than an eventual law practice. At any rate, he escaped law school after one year and headed to Stanford University to enter its graduate program in political science.

Following his headlong schedule to finish his education and get on with his career, Hatfield pushed quickly through a master's program in political science in 1947–48. Relying on GI funding, he worked diligently and full time at his graduate work, finishing up in summer 1948. He then continued for a year as a doctoral student before deciding to drop out to begin teaching at Willamette University and at the same time considering a career in politics.

Stanford at the time featured a strong faculty and a plethora of courses in its department of political science. During his two years there, Hatfield enrolled in courses in political theory, political parties, public administration, government organization, and international relations. Some of these subjects he would himself teach when he returned to Willamette as a faculty member in fall 1949.

The most demanding part of Hatfield's graduate program was the writing of his thesis. The director of the thesis was noted political scientist Thomas S. Barclay, who taught several later senators, including Hatfield, Frank Church, Lee Metcalf, Alan Cranston, and Henry "Scoop" Jackson. Barclay encouraged his students to become politically active, to travel to Washington, D.C., to see firsthand American politics at work. The professor was known for his lively lectures, spiced with humorous anecdotes he assiduously collected.

Not surprisingly, Hatfield chose to write a thesis on Herbert Hoover. As a longtime fan of Hoover, Hatfield also benefited in having a burgeoning collection of Hoover materials at Stanford. He would also make contact with the ex-president in researching and writing his thesis.

Hatfield's thesis, "Herbert Hoover and Labor: Policies and Attitudes, 1897–1928," reveals a good deal about Hatfield as a political thinker in his mid-twenties. Realizing Hatfield's strong attachment to Republican political stances, it is not surprising that his thesis on Hoover is largely sympathetic to the engineer's, cabinet member's, and president's stances on labor matters. More a narrative than an analytical and evaluative study, Hatfield's thesis explains Hoover's stress on local and state entities rather than the federal government

Mark Hatfield and President Herbert Hoover. While still a preteen, Hatfield became enamored with President Hoover. Later Hatfield led Hoover rallies, wrote a master's thesis on Hoover, and followed closely several of Hoover's key political ideas. Hatfield and Hoover photograph, GFU.01.09, George Fox University Photographs, George Fox University Archives, Newberg, Oregon.

as the agencies best able to handle tensions between owners and workers, on strikes, and other labor policies. Not until his conclusion does Hatfield raise the possibility that more federal government activity might have helped settle more labor-ownership conflicts. But there is no support here for the New Deal policies in the 1930s that brought the federal government into so many labor-management conflicts.

Besides completing his master's in political science, Hatfield made an important connection central to his later career. At Stanford, he became reacquainted with undergraduate Travis Cross, a friend from Salem. They quickly bonded and talked often about Oregon and political careers. When Oregon's governor, Earl Snell, secretary of state, Robert S. Farrell Jr., and senate president, Marshall E. Cornett, died in a plane crash in October 1947, the Hatfield-Cross conversations about possible political positions in Oregon moved to front and center. When a car wreck delayed Hatfield's schooling at Stanford and he turned down a staff offering at the University of Chicago, he returned to Salem in the summer of 1949 and explained his needs to President Smith of Willamette. The president, although having just hired a second faculty member to expand political science offerings, found a place for Hatfield. He offered Mark an instructor-ship in political science for a salary of $2,600. Cross was hired as campus director of information.

Once back on the Willamette campus, Hatfield, as usual, lost no time in becoming involved in new political ventures. Even though burdened with a heavy teaching load, he displayed that enormous fund of enthusiasm and energy for political matters. He and Travis Cross worked up a series of radio programs, *The Political Pulse*. The programs inter-viewed political leaders, commented on Oregon politics, and included Hatfield's opinions about these people and political events. He also gave several speeches supporting the Hoover Report (1949), which called for a return to the less federal government–driven years before Franklin Roosevelt and the New Deal. The report squared with the Republican ideas that percolated in Hatfield's mind. In addition, the new political science instructor was named chairman of the Young Republican Policy Committee of Oregon.

Repeatedly, as Hatfield talked on the radio, spoke at the Hoover Report meetings, and participated in Republican gatherings, he was encouraged to run for public office. Moving gradually in that direction, Mark decided in late 1949 he would run for the Oregon House of Representatives.

2

Oregon Politician, 1950–1958

It was late in 1950, a year of notable transition for the youthful Mark Hatfield. At age twenty-eight he had just completed his master's at Stanford and one year of teaching at his alma mater, Willamette University. Now he was moving in a new direction. Asking permission to do so from Willamette's President Smith, Hatfield had thrown his hat into the race to represent Marion County at Salem in the Oregon House of Representatives. Once that decision was made in early 1950, Hatfield became a full-throttle, upbeat, and successful political candidate, winning first place in the Republican primary and also first in the general election later in the fall. Mark Hatfield, until now an energetic student and aspiring politician, had transitioned from a hoped-for career to the beginning of a long one. He had become an elected politician, a role he would play nonstop without defeat for nearly a half century, first at state and then national levels.

A major conflict bedeviled Hatfield in the early 1950s. His commitment to an evangelical Christian path had wobbled and cooled in graduate school and his first months of teaching at Willamette. Then a direct challenge to his semidormant spiritual life came from devout students at the university. One of the student leaders, Doug Coe, raised a question or two about Hatfield's religious journey. The

Hatfield as professor and political candidate. In 1950–51, Hatfield served as professor of political science at Willamette University. He also became a successful candidate for the Oregon legislature. Photograph from Marion County Voters' Pamphlet, 1950.

searching questions spun Hatfield out of his lukewarm commitment, pushing him in 1953 to recommit himself to a strong, renewed evangelical path. The recommitment sent him headlong into a second struggle: how would he balance his new spiritual promises with the demands of his rising political dream. For the remainder of his public career, he had to deal with the ongoing challenges between faith and politics. The events of the 1950s had introduced the tension, but now, unlike that earlier time, Hatfield would not give way on his faith. He would work out a balance between his spirituality and his career in politics.

The election of 1950 officially launched Hatfield's political career. Willamette's president assented in allowing Hatfield to run for office, but he also requested that Hatfield serve as dean of students at the university. In these decisions—and the events that soon followed—Hatfield revealed his enormous fund of energy and mounting ambitions.

Hatfield's surprising election into the Oregon house came in the midst of one of the decided shifts in Oregon politics from the 1840s onward. Early on, so strong were the Democrats that in the Oregon Constitutional Convention of 1857 only fifteen of the sixty members were anti-Democrats. All the rest were Democrats, as was Oregon from the earliest immigrants up the Oregon Trail. Overnight the first political shift took place. Abraham Lincoln, the country's first Republican president, won a four-sided election in 1860 in Oregon and by a much larger margin in 1864. During the Reconstruction and Gilded Age years stretching up to the 1890s, and then in the decades up to the Depression in the next century, Republicans became the dominant party in Oregon. Horatio Seymour in 1868 and Woodrow Wilson in 1912 were the only Democrats able to win presidential elections in Oregon from Lincoln to Franklin Roosevelt in 1932. More Republicans than Democrats were also elected to the U.S. Senate and House of Representatives in this eighty-year period.

Oregon Republicans were not entirely unified, however. In the 1900–1920 period, reformer William S. U'Ren introduced a strong progressive element into the party with his successful push for the "Oregon System," including the "direct democracy" measures of the initiative, referendum, recall, and direct election of senators. Although the rise of the Ku Klux Klan in the 1920s complicated Republican leadership, the party remained in charge until the four elections of Franklin Roosevelt from 1932 to 1944. Even in the Roosevelt years, however, Republican voters outnumbered Democrats. Not until 1950, for the first time in the twentieth century, were more Democrats than Republicans registered in Oregon. That meant Hatfield was elected in a year when a shift toward the Democrats had begun. He would emerge and rise to the top of Oregon politics, as a Republican, in a period of expanding Democratic strength.

In 1950, Hatfield launched his candidacy in the nearby town of Silverton, where he would announce nearly all of his later runs for public office. An even more dramatic representation of Hatfield's candidacy broke out in Salem. Students, a few faculty members, and fetched-up band from a campus fraternity marched to the capitol to draw attention to Hatfield's candidacy. The fuss did exactly that, with residents turning out to see what was happening. And there was a photograph and story in the newspaper about Hatfield's run for office. In addition, Hatfield coauthored an article on the Republican Advance, a liberal branch of the Republican Party in the newly launched Republican magazine, *The Republican Statesman.*

Simultaneously, in his entry in the 1950 voters' pamphlet for the fall elections, Hatfield made a clear, strong case for his candidacy. He spoke of his home and his religious, educational, and military backgrounds, particularly those related to his Oregon ties. He also listed his political experiences as a chairman of the Hoover Report, his service for the Republican Party, his teaching of political science and government courses, and his work with the radio program dealing with local politics. Hatfield could not brag of previous office-holding, but he could point to several specific experiences in local politics. And he promised he would show "responsibility and trust, always living up to the confidence placed in him by others."

Hatfield faced eleven other Republican candidates in the spring primary. Later, in the fall general election, four Democrats and three other Republicans were competitors. As a newcomer, having never run for public office, Hatfield decided early on that he would launch a campaign different from that of many other candidates. It would be a political strategy he would follow for more than four decades.

Hatfield and campaign manager Travis Cross, also on the staff at Willamette University, realized they "had to do things differently." Other political aspirants might use abundant funding to propel their political races, but Hatfield and his lieutenants decided they would "mobilize people" rather than rely on campaign monies. They would "know citizens and let them know me." This one-on-one strategy of meeting voters face to face, as much as possible, was Hatfield's goal and plan beginning with his first run for public office.

It was an endless, energy-consuming plan. Traditional political canvasses latched on to leading citizens such as bankers, lawyers, and other notables and worked through them to capture other voters. In contrast, Hatfield set out to be "a Populist, shaking hands and listening to as many people as I could rather than relying on campaign literature or distant handbills." The Hatfield style of office seeking meant a nonstop, day-after-day run of meetings and speeches. Sometimes he cajoled local citizens to walk with him in the streets of their communities, chatting with as many townspeople as possible, introducing himself to any and all residents. It might have been billed a "getting-to-know them" campaign plan—for both the office seeker and the voter.

The door-to-door, handshake-to-handshake, and talk-to-everybody system worked—and functioned extraordinarily well. In both the primary and general elections in 1950, Hatfield was the top vote getter. In the November runoffs, three other Republicans and Hatfield won seats in the Oregon house. The voting totals were Hatfield, 19,566; Lee Ohmart, 18,764; Roy L. Houck, 18,608; John F. Steelhammer, 16,392. The four winners, including Hatfield, were all Salem residents. The four Democrats trailed the Republicans; no Democrat won a house seat from the Twelfth District, stretching down from Portland on the western side of the Willamette Valley.

Now that Hatfield was officially a new member of the Oregon House of Representatives, he had to decide where he would stand on the stage of state politics. Obviously he was a Republican, but he had to wrestle with what kind of Republican he would be. That was not an easy decision for Hatfield, nor has it been for historians, biographers, and political commentators trying to categorize Hatfield's positions in his nearly half century of state and national politics.

Most of the indicators, over time, revealed that Hatfield swung neither to the right or left. Still, through the years he was labeled, variously, as a radical, liberal, or progressive leaning left or a traditionalist or conservative leaning right—and sometimes, by more middle-of-the-road descriptors, as a moderate or independent. Interestingly, Hatfield used the words "libertarian," "radical," and "rebel" in defining his stances, although his definitions of those words were not consonant with wider uses of the words. Also, some of his political positions changed over time. Most have thought his political stances were clearer in Oregon than during his long years as a U.S. senator. From his first election in 1950 until his reelection as governor in 1962, Hatfield gradually defined his Republican and other political positions.

Hatfield's workload obviously became much more demanding in 1950–51. He continued as a political science instructor during the year, but at the end of July he accepted President Smith's invitation to become Willamette's dean of students. Then, in January 1951, he became a member of the state legislature and had to add those time-consuming duties to his already heavy load. The university worked out a schedule so that Hatfield taught his courses between eight and ten and was on the floor of the Oregon house when it was called to order at ten A.M. A munificent $600 was added to Hatfield's salary as a new legislator.

Even though at this time Hatfield summarized his experiences as a navy man, a professor of political science, and his backgrounds as a home-grown Oregonian, he did not announce a specific political agenda on the way to the house of representatives. His appearance in the Thirty-Sixth Oregon Legislative Assembly drew some attention, but other matters were even more noted. At twenty-eight he was the youngest member of the house and the first professor to serve in more than thirty years. One journalist also called him the most handsome of the new representatives. Another journalist, Richard Neuberger, named Hatfield one of "the most promising" of the legislative newcomers. Hatfield and the Republicans dominated the house, holding fifty-one of the sixty seats, and twenty-one of thirty in the senate. Attracting even more comment were the first husband-and-wife team, Richard (in the senate) and Maurine (in the house) Neuberger, to serve in the legislature.

Hatfield was assigned to several committees, most of which dovetailed with his interests and expertise. He would serve on the Elections Committee, out of which came several of his legislative pushes. He was given a seat on the Education Committee, where he expressed his opinions about school funding and the possible status of Portland State College (University). Most important for the future was his role on the State and Federal Affairs Committee.

Several major issues faced the ninety Oregon legislators, none more pressing than the state's in-the-red economy. The deficit had ballooned from $6.5 million facing the previous legislature to $61 million in 1951. In the longest ever to-date legislature, stretching for 116 days, the legislators were able, through budget reductions and a few tax measures, to cut the deficit in half. But red ink continued to flow in the early 1950s.

Hatfield, in his later accounts, did not comment on the deficit issue. Instead he focused on a controversial, stand-alone decision he made early on. Hatfield summed up his actions as "reaffirm[ing] the strength of convictions." The issue dealt with oleo, a white margarine substitute for butter, which was difficult to secure during wartime. Dairy farmers hated it when the white oleo was precolored yellow; for them, the yellow oleo would be a harmful competitor to authentic butter. Hatfield, however, voted for the precolored oleo even though many of his agricultural voters adamantly opposed it. He concluded he had done the right thing in spite of the opposition of so many voters who might not support him again.

Hatfield introduced or supported several other bills. He helped initiate a bill that would allow the time extension of school indebtedness but voted against another transferring jurisdiction of the state police to a new six-man board. He also supported legislation for the state to reimburse those using their own vehicles for state work and voted for a few needed tax revenues. In education matters, Hatfield cosigned a bill that required "teachers to sign non-Communist affidavits." More important, he stood for Senate Bill 211, supported by both Richard and Maurine Neuberger, calling for a convention to rewrite the lengthy, cumbersome state constitution.

The issues that most attracted Hatfield, however, were those around possible reapportionment, the manner in which representatives were selected for the state house and senate. This subject had captured Hatfield's attention before he was elected to the legislature in 1950. While a leader in the nascent Young Republicans previous to January 1951, Hatfield had helped mastermind a new method of choosing members of the legislature. His plans dealt with the political representation challenges stretching all the way back to the writing of the U.S. Constitution: how were congressional representatives to be chosen, by a state-by-state selection or by population? A compromise system resulted: two members from each state for the Senate and numbers in the House based on state populations. Hatfield thought that plan better than the one Oregon was currently following in 1950–51.

Not all versions of the reapportionment bill that Hatfield supported were the same, but they essentially called for representation to be based more on population than it had been. Some versions even suggested senatorial representation to be determined by numbers. In the midst of the heated reapportionment discussions, Hatfield reminded his fellow house members of their promise to uphold the state constitution, which called for "decennial reapportionment," even though that guideline had not been followed for forty years. Hatfield was outspoken on this point: "The philosophy of belittling the constitution has spread like an infectious disease in the last 15 years."

Hatfield voiced the views of those who wanted representation to be reapportioned, to be based more explicitly on recent population shifts. Those with this perspective were in the minority in the house. The majority views came from the rural areas, especially from residents east of the Cascades who benefited from the current apportionment guidelines based on earlier population figures. The house killed Hatfield's idea 38 to 21. Disappointed, Hatfield did not give up on his wish; he continued his call for reapportionment in years to come.

In subsequent writings, Hatfield did not provide a summing up of his first legislative experience in 1951. Others, on the other hand, furnished comments about Hatfield and his political engagement. In September 1950 before the legislature opened in January 1951, Hatfield had urged the Young Republicans in a combined meeting to end the group's "present negative Republican policy toward the [Truman] administration and establish a positive and constructive alternative to every issue on which we differ with the Democrats." As an *Oregonian* reporter noted, this recommendation was "roundly applauded" and distanced Hatfield from the more conservative members of his group. Another journalist added that Hatfield "has a sound and progressive record in the younger circles of the [Republican] party and may be relied upon to acquit himself with independence and vigor." The next month another journalist saluted Hatfield as a "liberal," one of the "aggressive liberals" of the Young Republicans. After the legislature completed its work in spring 1951, the *Oregon Voter* was even more emphatic in praise of Hatfield. "As a first-termer, he [Hatfield] made an excellent showing . . . a fine personality . . . exceptionally able in floor debate . . . clear in exposition." Obviously Hatfield was winning considerable attention among his colleagues and in the newspapers for his political activities and leadership in 1950–51.

The state legislature had scarcely closed its doors in May 1951 before Hatfield zipped on to his next political activity. Beginning in summer 1951 and for nearly a year, he was the nonstop cheerleader for the nomination of General Dwight D. Eisenhower as the Republican presidential candidate in Oregon. In fact, even before the legislature completed its work, Hatfield had begun to pound the drum for Eisenhower. Hatfield began his push for "Ike" antecedent to the lionized military leader declaring himself either a Republican or a Democrat. For Hatfield, Eisenhower promised to be the ideal candidate, less a stick-in-the-mud conservative like Senator Robert A. Taft of Ohio or the possibly too liberal Earl Warren, governor of California.

When the legislature completed its work in May and classes at Willamette were finished in early summer, Hatfield went full bore on his Eisenhower activities. Still, before he was able to gather the needed thousand petition signatures to put Eisenhower's name on the Oregon Republican ballot, Democrats were already at work, announcing in July that they had gathered numerous names to a petition asking that Eisenhower be placed as a Democrat on the Oregon ballot.

The lively competition between the Democrats and Republicans was all the more unusual because Eisenhower had not yet declared to which party he belonged. In late

July, Hatfield said he would hold off filing his Republican petitions until Eisenhower revealed his party affiliation and not until he had secured petition signatures from every part of Oregon. The next month when the Democrats filed 1,150 signatures to place Eisenhower on the Oregon ballot, Hatfield seemed unconcerned and was convinced the general would come out as a Republican. When Senator Henry Cabot Lodge stated the next January that Eisenhower was a Republican (Eisenhower had not so stated publicly), the Oregon Republicans were euphoric. Hatfield, now executive secretary of the Oregon-for-Eisenhower group, called Lodge's statement "of great note." But the Eisenhower petition would not yet be submitted, because signatures from all parts of Oregon had not been secured. When Eisenhower admitted his Republican candidacy and allowed his name to be filed in the New Hampshire primary, his presidential candidacy was now certain, and the Republican petition was submitted in Oregon for his White House run.

As the election of 1952 began to heat up nationally, an intriguing, revealing division erupted among Oregon Republicans. Party delegates met in Salem prior to the Republican national convention in Chicago in July; their purpose, to select a delegate as Oregon's representative to the party's national convention platform committee. Amazingly, Senator Wayne Morse was not selected. Instead, Mark Hatfield was, winning over Morse 13 to 5. In his book *Not Quite So Simple*, Hatfield presented a semihumorous explanation of the vote: the vote, via his "more accurate" interpretation, was "5 votes for Morse, 1 for Hatfield (I voted for myself) and 12 votes against Morse." Hatfield's interpretation was on track, for Morse had begun to alienate his more conservative Republican colleagues. He left the Republicans in 1952, became an independent, and joined the Democrats in 1955.

Controversies of another kind embroiled Hatfield the next month at the Chicago convention. As members of the platform committee, he, John Foster Dulles, and Christian Herter tried to revise and strengthen a weak, inadequate statement on civil rights in the Republican platform. The dictatorial committee chairman, Senator Eugene Milliken of Colorado, brushed by Roberts' Rules of Order and gaveled down the possible civil rights plank. At the time, the convention supporters of presidential hopeful Robert A. Taft had control of the convention and defeated the attempt to bring in the civil rights revision.

In 1952, Hatfield ran for reelection to the Oregon house. In the spring, he easily won the primary and in November the general election as well. A number of factors, possibly in this order, figured into his reelection: (1) his strong performance in the house in 1951; (2) his rising notoriety in Republican ranks, especially in the push for and success of the Eisenhower candidacy; (3) his party's strength in Oregon, including forty-nine of sixty in the house and twenty-six of thirty in the senate, plus all four U.S. House seats and the governor's chair; (4) the presidential turnout for Eisenhower in Oregon (61 percent) over the Democrat Adlai Stevenson (39 percent); and (5) the ongoing division in the Democratic Party between individualistic, personal-gain conservatives and more progressive Roosevelt, Truman, and New Deal and Fair Deal liberals.

Several observers commented on Hatfield's popularity as a youthful, budding politician. He was the leading vote getter in the primary and general elections of the four representatives from Marion County in 1954, as he had been in 1952. Hatfield's close friend and political supporter Travis Cross, in a full-page story about Hatfield in the 29 June 1952 issue of the *Oregonian,* undoubtedly meaning to boost Hatfield between the primary and general elections, concluded that Hatfield's campaign was going "off without a hitch." Another commentator, playing with names and words, wrote "'It looks like Mark is made.' At least, he has made a mark in the Oregon political scene." Still another author, writing later for the *Saturday Evening Post*, pointed out that the hidebound, old-time Republicans were not inviting Hatfield into the smoke-filled inner circles of the party, but they failed to realize that he "was attracting to himself a group of dedicated, selfless followers who believed implicitly in his future." In yet another story in the *Oregonian*, a reporter noted Hatfield's mounting reputation as a young man putting in sixteen-hour days as a professor yet seeming to do well as a legislator. "Being a bachelor," Hatfield told the journalist, "his time . . . [was] his own, so no explanations were necessary."

The Forty-Seventh Oregon Legislative Assembly stretched out one hundred days, from 12 January to 21 April 1953. In all, 747 bills were passed, an average of more than seven per day, with another 556 going down to defeat. Although fallout from the Korean War and the McCarthy controversies were roiling the nation, the Oregon representatives in Salem, unlike those gathered in Sacramento to the south and Olympia to the north, focused on other pressing issues. The major challenge was as before—how to handle burgeoning state debts, what tax programs to implement, and how to address the most critical financial needs. Closely related were other dilemmas, including declining economic growth and high unemployment. Hatfield participated in attempts to solve these economic challenges, but his major interests and activities were in other areas.

In the 1953 legislature, Hatfield served on several committees, including Education, Elections and Reapportionment, Bills and Mailing, and as chairman of State and Federal Affairs. One of his chief concerns had been addressed even before the legislature convened. Hatfield's steady push for reapportionment clearly helped lead to a constitutional amendment being placed on the ballot the previous November. Oregon voters overwhelmingly supported the legislation calling for decennial reapportionment of voting districts for the two chambers. If the legislature failed in carrying out the redistricting, the secretary of state would be required to do so. The reapportionment decision was a pleasing moment for Hatfield.

Hatfield was involved in several legislative enactments. Ones that he supported but made little of were a measure to secure a governor's mansion in Salem, added highway funding, and rewriting several state laws. On the other hand, he did not support liquor-by-the-drink or a state measure for what would become Portland State University. The legislature passed both of the latter bills.

Two other legislative enactments very much involved Hatfield. He worked closely with Governor Paul Patterson to introduce a bill calling for a constitutional convention to rewrite or greatly revise the Oregon constitution. Hatfield had supported the proposed bill in the previous legislature, but neither body was able to get Oregonians to back the idea.

Perhaps the legislation that meant most to Hatfield, at least that he later emphasized, was a civil rights measure. He explained his support for the legislation through personal experiences. When he was a student leader at Willamette and the university hosted African American performers Paul Robeson and Marian Anderson, neither he nor the university was able to find public accommodations for the artists. The Salem hotels maintained a "No Coloreds" policy, and thus Hatfield had to drive the performers to Portland for a place to stay. To correct this injustice, Hatfield, as chairman of the State and Federal Affairs Committee, worked closely with Speaker of the House Rudie Wilhelm to introduce a bill on public accommodations. The civil rights legislation became "the spotlight of the entire session." Previous similar efforts had failed, with many Salem hotel owners and beverage outlets and motels throughout the state opposed to the proposed Hatfield bill.

Hatfield set out to win passage of the civil rights bill by contacting fellow legislators one by one to secure their

Hatfield and civil rights. Hatfield began his support for civil rights as a college student. Later, as a state legislator, he encouraged passage of Oregon's Civil Rights Bill in 1953. Here he joins other supporters of the Civil Rights Bill. Oregon Historical Society, OrHi 44402.

support and vote. It was not an easy task, because Oregon had a tradition of racial discrimination, all the way back to the writing of its constitution in 1857 and the infamous "sundown laws" maintained illegally in the twentieth century. Still, Hatfield and his supporters achieved their goal; the legislature passed the public housing laws banning racial discrimination in public accommodations. For Hatfield it was a huge achievement: "I gained arguably one of the great victories of my entire career." Or, as he put it on another occasion, "During that session I helped pass one of the bills I remain most proud of throughout almost 50 years of public service. And well beyond."

As the legislature pushed on in 1953 and Hatfield's influence was increasingly evident, a few supporters were pressing him to think of running for higher office. Some suggested competing for a seat in the U.S. House of Representatives. Hatfield did not respond to these suggestions, but thoughts about other political posts probably were percolating, even though he did not mention them.

Two other happenings in 1952–53 proved eventually life-altering. In 1952, Hatfield met Antoinette Kuzmanich for the first time. The daughter of a Yugoslavian father and a Portland mother, Antoinette was then twenty-three years old. She became a high school English teacher and later, after gaining a master's at Stanford, served as a women's counselor and then dean of women at Portland State University. She and Mark met off and on, including her participation in a two-month European tour that Mark directed. Once Antoinette returned from Stanford in 1955, the romance between the two of them accelerated, but off scene. Then they announced their engagement in 1957, and marriage followed in July 1958 during Hatfield's successful run for the governorship. Eventually they became the parents of four children, with Antoinette winning accolades as wife, mother, political supporter, and hostess. Hatfield often referred to Antoinette as his strongest lifetime supporter. They were married for fifty-three years.

The other transformative happening was more a gradual spiritual awakening than a specific event. As dean of students at Willamette, Hatfield was often called upon to listen to and counsel a variety of students. By 1954 he was feeling increasingly uncomfortable about these sessions when students turned to him for religious guidance. He wondered if his genuine spiritual tank was not running on low. It was not that he had been inactive in evangelical circles; he continued as a leader in Salem's First Baptist Church and was participating in such well-known evangelical groups as Youth for

Christ, Campus Crusade, and World Vision. In one year he gave seventeen presentations to religious organizations and conventions, including Assemblies of God, Nazarene, and Baptist churches.

Still, as Lon Fendall points out in his revealing study of Hatfield's religious life and political career, *Stand Alone or Come Home* (2008), Hatfield felt as "a-spiritual as they [his students] were a-political." "He began to see," Fendall continues, "his spirituality as external, routine, and uncommitted." The discontent came to a head when one student, Doug Coe, asked for permission to launch a Bible study, which Hatfield allowed. But when Coe went on to ask deeper questions about Hatfield's own religious journey, the dean was embarrassed that he could not give satisfying answers—to Coe or himself. That realization set Hatfield on a journey of spiritual recovery. From then on, he more diligently and personally invested himself in religious matters. The container of genuine spiritual devotion had begun refilling.

In 1954, Hatfield remained busy at teaching full time and running for a new office. After some indecision, in March he had announced his candidacy for the state senate. Hatfield and his colleague from the Oregon house, Lee Ohmart, would take on incumbent Douglas Yeater, also a Republican like Hatfield and Ohmart. In announcing his run for the senate, Hatfield included support for a new state constitution. In the May primary he topped the list of Marion County candidates for the fifth straight time; he and Ohmart were elected, with Yeater "placing a very bad third" in the contest for the two senate seats.

After the two-month hiatus in Europe traveling with and teaching college undergraduates, Hatfield returned to politicking and running toward the coming general election in November. In September at a Republican Club meeting in Portland, he urged his listeners "to work aggressively" in the political arena. "Take the offense," he told them, "and let the other side be on the defensive." He also turned more partisan than usual in pointed criticisms of the Democrats. The sharpest shots were saved for Wayne Morse, whom Hatfield did not name but obviously referred to. "Remember . . . we (Republicans) a few years ago were taken in by an outspoken man. We sent him to Washington. After a few years he became an independent." Moving on, Hatfield warned further to "be careful . . . of those who are too anxious to trumpet their own horn." The tension between Hatfield and Morse was heating up.

After easily winning election to the Oregon Senate in November, Hatfield continued his criticism of Morse and other Democrats. He pointed to what he considered Senator Morse's illegal use of government franking privileges to send out Christmas cards to voters. He accused Morse of wrongly employing "government expense for the 1956 election" in the card sending. Republicans needed to be careful of Morse because of his "shuttlecock activities in the U.S. Senate."

Hatfield's run for the senate seat occurred amid another shift in the Oregon political landscape. In the fall 1954 elections the Democrats flexed their expanding political muscle. Democrat Richard Neuberger won a seat in the U.S. Senate by defeating incumbent Republican Guy Condon; Democrat Edith Green won a U.S. House seat over Republican Tom McCall; and Democratic numbers in the Oregon house jumped from eleven to twenty-five, in the state senate from four to six. Republican Hatfield was an exception to these Democratic surges.

Soon after the November general election, Hatfield made clear his continuing support for one of his favorite measures. In its final two-year meeting, the Constitutional Revision Committee voted to submit both majority and minority reports for a possible bill to the 1955 legislature. Hatfield voted with the majority to call for a constitutional convention to carry out a total revision of what he considered a poorly written, cumbersome state constitution. The minority report urged, instead, a piecemeal move of revision. Hatfield's support for the larger revision continued during the next year.

When Hatfield took his seat in the Oregon Senate in January 1955, he faced working with different colleagues, serving on new committees, and dealing with issues from other perspectives. The challenges seemed to make little difference; Hatfield rose as quickly to senate leadership as he had in the house from 1951 to 1953. In fact, in the year's time from his election to the senate to his announcement for secretary of state in late 1955, Hatfield seemed nonstop in teaching, serving in the legislature, and speaking several times nearly every month. His name was everywhere in the state's newspapers.

The 1955 legislature convened on Monday, 10 January, and lasted until 4 May. In those 114 days of hectic meetings, 774 of 1,132 bills passed the legislature. Most of the legislation, as expected, dealt with state matters, but a few bills also treated national or even global issues.

Hatfield's senate committee assignments both duplicated and broke from his work in the Oregon house. He was named chairman of the State and Federal Affairs Committee, the same committee on which he had served in the house. In another duplication of house experiences, he was named to the Education Committee, on which he served as vice chair. Other committees for Hatfield were Public Health, Resolutions, and Natural Resources. In none of these did he seem to be very active or to gain much publicity.

The senate moved quickly. On opening day it introduced twenty-six bills and had begun to process them before closing later that day. Hatfield introduced two possible constitutional amendments, one, not surprisingly, calling for a constitutional convention to revise or rewrite the state's constitution; it was similar to what he had introduced from the house in 1953. The other Hatfield bill urged the senate to formulate a constitutional amendment that would lower the voting age from twenty-one to eighteen. Both would gain a good deal of discussion in the coming months. Another bill Hatfield introduced would raise teachers' minimum salaries at all levels of educational preparation—from those without a bachelor's degree to holders of a master's.

Hatfield's push for a constitutional convention in 1959 was the first of his measures to gain focus. The senate discussions immediately revealed how divided the senators were on the proposal. The majority of the eleven-member committee discussing the possible convention voted in its favor, but then other members spoke for—and got—a minority report calling not for a convention but for an amendment-by-amendment revision in the legislature. Hatfield introduced the majority committee report, which had the support of Republican governor Paul Patterson, but divisions within the committee resurfaced later in the full senate and eventually doomed the measure even though, at times, it seemed a majority favored a constitutional convention. The defeat of the measure was a clear disappointment to Hatfield.

Hatfield's brief stint in the Oregon Senate included his most active support of educational measures during his legislative years. He spoke several times in committee and on the senate floor for legislation to raise teacher's salaries. Most of his senate colleagues supported the general idea of a salary enhancement, although a few Portlanders fretted about being able to secure sufficient funding to cover the raises. Eventually a compromise was reached, pushing beginning teacher salaries up from $2,100 to $3,000. Had the new funding been immediately available, 1,727 teachers across Oregon would have gained higher salaries.

Hatfield participated in several other education measures. He introduced a bill to "give state scholarships to needy students." Later in the session, he also supported Portland State's becoming a four-year, state-funded college (he had opposed the move in previous legislative sessions) but worried about the new college's impact on nearby private colleges, probably including his Willamette University, perhaps the University of Portland, and maybe even George Fox and Warner Pacific colleges. He also voted for budget measures that added decisively to state support for public education.

The most surprising Hatfield moves in his senate days were his mounting criticisms of Senator Wayne Morse. The unusual part is not that Morse's actions were undeserving of criticisms but that Hatfield was a chief critic. For the most part Hatfield had refrained from firing off broadsides at Morse or any other opponent. Earlier, too, he had been a supporter of Morse when the latter began his U.S. Senate career. But Hatfield's tack then changed, beginning with aforementioned criticisms in December 1954 and extending on into Hatfield's state senate months in 1955.

Hatfield's negative comments on Morse seemed to derive from two major sources. He was upset, first of all, that Morse had abandoned the Republicans, become an independent, and announced his conversion to the Democrats in the Lane County courthouse in Eugene on 18 February 1955. Hearing of the switch, Hatfield labeled Morse "'the political Hamlet,' because he kept saying 'to be or not to be' for 28 months." Hatfield asserted, too, that Morse's political move called for the "exodus from the Democratic party those who are alert to the Trojan horse [Morse] which has been wheeled into their midst by their state chairman [Howard Morgan]." These comments were but prologue to the heated verbal conflicts that ensued between Hatfield and Morse in coming years.

Another subject that captured Hatfield's backing and leadership was the call to lower the voting age. He had introduced the measure to the senate's Resolutions Committee. The resolution set off conflicting reactions, even among young people in the age gap. Hatfield asserted that denying voting rights to those under age twenty-one was a hangover of "feudalistic tradition" from English common law that was meaningless for modern Americans. Modern opinion polls had shown, Hatfield added, that a majority of Americans favored the voting age reduction. Interestingly, young people between the ages of eighteen and twenty-one who testified before the Resolutions Committee were divided on the measure. Some thought the move good and long overdue; others asserted that eighteen-year-olds were not yet ready to vote. Opponents added that young people needed the added time to experience more of life, to understand more about their responsibilities, before they were invited to the ballot box. Hatfield continued to push for the measure while in the Oregon Senate.

Nearly all of the senate activities in 1955 linked to Mark Hatfield were Oregon matters. A few, however, dealt with national or even global topics. On several occasions Hatfield praised what he thought to be President Eisenhower's balance and nonpartisan stances. Of note, Hatfield did not comment on the notable Supreme Court case of 1954, *Brown v. Board of Education of Topeka*, which called for the end of school segregation. He said little, too, about McCarthyism, anticommunism, and the civil rights boycotts roiling the nation in the mid-1950s.

One intriguing set of Hatfield comments emerged from controversies surrounding President Eisenhower's so-called Formosa Resolution. This congressional action in late January 1955 authorized President Eisenhower to protect offshore Formosa (Taiwan) from an attack from mainland Communist China. Hatfield described Eisenhower's actions in this regard as an "act of peace," meaning cordial relations between the president and Congress. When a Republican colleague of Hatfield's criticized Wayne Morse for not supporting the Formosa action, the Oregon Senate exploded into a furious debate about loyalty, political rightness, and misguided actions.

A few other Hatfield actions as a state senator did not capture as much attention. His successful support for a bill calling for the abolishment of wage discrimination between the sexes received mention but nothing more. Hatfield discussed a much different issue in a debate of several bills attempting to outlaw sex crime publications, especially sales to persons age eighteen and younger. Hatfield objected to some of the most inclusive of these bills because they failed "to distinguish between what is art and what is low-brow entertainment when it comes to consideration of obscenity." Hatfield had entered that age-old controversy between the treatment of controversial subjects like sex and violence in works of high art on one side and "lowbrow obscenity" on the other. The discussion seemed not to satisfy those wanting prohibition of the books or a silenced Hatfield.

Once the senate session ended in early May, Hatfield finished the school year and went on the road making speeches all over Oregon in the next few months. By early fall, rumors floated that he might run for a statewide office. In his first years in politics, Hatfield seemed to keep his eyes continually open for possible advancement. Such a change became clear in late 1955. The incumbent secretary of state, Earl T. Newbry, was not legally eligible to be reelected, so Hatfield jumped into the race for secretary of state on 17 November 1955. He also realized that he could not keep up with two full-time jobs and announced that he would not renew his teaching contract with Willamette after summer 1956.

In his announcement, Hatfield made three pledges to Oregon voters. He assured an "integrity and personal faithfulness to duty" if elected; he would "support further reorganization of state departments to achieve added efficiency"; and he would "lend sympathetic understanding to the administration of state institutions as a member of the board of control." On first glance, these promises might have seemed simply political shoptalk, but those who knew Hatfield and his track record in the legislature during the past half-dozen years could see reiteration of his past promises and achievements.

Hatfield quickly expanded his campaigning to statewide politicking, away from the Marion County–focused strategies of his senate years. He began to form a political team that would help him campaign throughout the state; several members of the team would later work with him in the offices of secretary of state and governor. His campaign slogan was "The ability to get things done . . . The courage to act"—again, words that might sound hollow to those off the scene, but clear, to the point, and obvious to those who knew Hatfield's previous political path.

Although Hatfield easily won the Republican primary in spring 1956, the general election in the fall proved to be a much closer race. Hatfield (147,896 votes) comfortably defeated fellow Republican William Healy (88,710 votes) in the spring runoff, while his Democratic opponent-to-be, Monroe Sweetland, ran unopposed in his party. Then the comparisons and contrasts between the Republican and Democratic candidates began to emerge. Their political positions in Oregon were very similar: like Hatfield, Sweetland had served two terms in the house and had just completed a term in the senate when he decided to run for secretary of state in 1955–56. The two had served together for these six years.

On specific issues, the two rising stars were quite different. Hatfield reflected his allegiance to Republican stances in his calls for power and strength at the local and state levels and the avoidance of too much concentration of force in the central government, which he believed had happened in the Roosevelt and Truman administrations. On the other hand, in his rise to leadership in Oregon, Sweetland had supported strong central governments and social programs, so strong and so many that his critics called Sweetland a socialist in his leadership of the Commonwealth Federation in the late 1930s and 1940s. Sweetland was the target of numerous criticisms, but Hatfield stayed away, for the most part, from the negative attacks on his Democratic opponent.

In fall 1956, Hatfield seemed to be forging ahead ever so slightly. When the *Oregonian,* the state's most influential newspaper, came out for Hatfield in October, it spoke of the political competition as "a clear test between a progressive Republican, Mark O. Hatfield, and a dedicated New Deal Democrat, Monroe Sweetland." But the paper went on to state a view that many Sweetland critics had adopted: he had a tendency toward socialism and had been "secretary of the far-left Commonwealth Federation." These backgrounds suggested that Sweetland, if elected, might lean clearly to the left. Others went even farther to label Sweetland a closet communist, or nearly so.

In his race for secretary of state, Hatfield was running against a rising Democratic tide. Wayne Morse, now a Democrat, beat Eisenhower's former secretary of the interior, Douglas McKay, and won reelection to the U.S. Senate. Democrat Robert Holmes defeated incumbent Elmo Smith for the governor's chair, and Democrats also secured three of the representative positions in the U.S. House. The Democrats also gained control of the Oregon legislature, the first time since 1878. Registered Democrats in Oregon now outnumbered Republicans 450,122 to 413,220.

Despite these countergains, Hatfield bested Democrat Sweetland for secretary of state. It was by no means a landslide or even large defeat, however. In fact, it was Hatfield's closest election; he won by less than 1 percent, pulling in 368,127 votes compared to Sweetland's 349,484. Hatfield's large majority in Marion County, his home country, was a big part of his slim victory over Sweetland.

Hatfield saw the secretary of state position as an opportunity to move beyond his six years of legislative experience into the new realm of an executive position. In hindsight, realizing how much he had learned in his two years as secretary of state and later applied in his eight years as governor, his perceptions about the secretary of state position were dead center and extremely valuable. As usual, Hatfield was planning and shaping his future well before entering that future.

Within a week after his election to become Oregon's secretary of state, Hatfield was making promises, laying out general plans, and beginning an office team that would carry over to his years as governor. A few days after he won the election, Hatfield spoke at Bend at the annual banquet of the Oregon Young Republicans. He laid out a three-point agenda for "party revitalization." Since Democrats had punched out the lights of the Republicans in the November elections, Hatfield's party, and he among them, was looking for ways to reunite and ignite a more successful political future. First of all, Hatfield told his listeners, the Republicans had to "build with idealism not upon organization and personalities alone but upon . . . what the individual citizen expects of his government." Second, the party must find and nominate "young, intelligent, articulate candidates" who could speak the language and think the thoughts "of their fellow citizens." Third, Oregon Republicans should embrace the "modern Republicanism" of President Eisenhower for a "constructive and progressive program" for Oregon. Though very general, these pragmatic suggestions remained central to Hatfield's thinking during the next few years.

By the end of December 1956, Hatfield had assembled part of his crew who became longtime members of his state and national staffs. For assistant secretary of state, he named Warne Nunn, who recently had served as director of the motor vehicle department after several other administrative assignments in Oregon government. Earlier in the month, Hatfield had appointed his friend Travis Cross to another administrative slot in the secretary of state's office. For office secretaries, Hatfield selected Leolyn Barnett and Lois Siegmund. Barnett had served beforehand as assistant

Hatfield's early staff. As secretary of state and governor, and later as U.S. senator, Hatfield gathered strong staff members. Here is an early group of advisors: (left to right) Travis Cross, Loren Hicks, and Warne Nunn. Image courtesy of Willamette University Archives and Special Collections.

to Secretary of State Earl Snell, and Siegmund had been Hatfield's secretary during his legislative years. This group, plus Gerry Frank and several others later, became the core of Hatfield's smooth-functioning office staff.

The opening weeks of 1957 revealed how Hatfield's administrative path in state politics would differ from his work in the legislature. In his most important administrative role, Hatfield served on the three-person Board of Control, along with Democratic governor Holmes and Republican state treasurer Sig Unander. Although Holmes presided at the board meetings, he was often outvoted two to one by the two Republicans. Over the next few months, tensions between the two political parties often popped up in Control Board decisions.

Those conflicts began to emerge early in 1957 in dealing with state institutions. For instance, in the first meeting of the board in January, Hatfield and Unander expressed their satisfaction with warden Clarence Gladden of the state prison, whereas Governor Holmes wanted to replace the warden with his own appointee. Other differences arose in the handling of the MacLaren home for boys. Some of the home's administrators wished to build a second school for boys so as to separate the older and younger residents. Hatfield disagreed. The keys to improvement, he argued, were not a second school but more counseling and stronger discipline. One journalist described Hatfield's position as "close to the problem [MacLaren] and studying the delinquent program closely."

If some of Hatfield's actions on the Control Board might have seemed "political" to Democrats, it was in other efforts that Hatfield more explicitly flew his political colors. Throughout the months of 1957 and 1958, he spoke at numerous Republican meetings, cheering on his party members but also pointing to ways the party might become stronger competitors against the Democrats. He urged his fellow Republicans to realize that "the president's coat tails alone are not enough for victory," as the Democratic victories in the election of 1956 "should have taught" them. In addition, he urged Republicans to stop "lone wolf" campaigning. His party members must push beyond differences displayed in primary contests and understand again "that best results are obtained by each member of a ticket supporting all others." When this team spirit was reignited and topped with "courage," the Republicans would be at their best.

Not surprisingly, Hatfield's support for his own party sometimes spilled over into criticism of the Democrats. In an atypical letter to the editor on 14 August 1957, he pointed out that the motor vehicle department was no longer lodged in his bailiwick but had been transferred to a separate division, with the director being appointed by the Democratic governor. The tensions between Hatfield and Governor Holmes would increase as 1957 and then 1958 wore on.

A few of Hatfield's political comments, his critics thought, smacked of self-congratulation. He spoke approvingly— critics implied bragged—of how under his leadership the office quarters of the secretary of state had corrected a waste of space, watched carefully any calls for new spending, and looked forward to launch new and better uses of the capitol malls. One reporter enjoyed punning with Hatfield's name— "Hatfield Sees Marked Gain"—in summarizing Hatfield's account of his accomplishments as secretary of state.

Fellow Republicans and opposing Democrats seemed unaware of how much attention Hatfield's nonstop speech making was gathering. In some weeks, Hatfield's presentations numbered three or four talks, and almost no week went by without a Hatfield presentation being announced. There were, of course, the political talks to the Young Republicans and other GOP groups. There were others for business groups and church organizations. Most notably were the number of speeches before women's gatherings. More than a reporter or two chuckled about Hatfield's attraction as one of the state's most eligible bachelors. What seemed overlooked was how much these speeches kept Hatfield before Oregon voters and in the newspapers. Perhaps Hatfield comprehended, and others did not, that these numerous presentations were as advertisements of his multitalents as a politician, speaker, and thinker. In every way, Hatfield's notices far outranked those of other Republicans and even Governor Holmes. In toto, in his first year in the secretary of state office, Hatfield had made 118 speeches, sat at the head table at invited meals 252 times, and had declined 400 invitations for other presentations.

In the opening weeks of 1958, in-the-moment politics shoved aside reports on Hatfield's activities as secretary of state. He announced his intention to run for Oregon's governor. Even before him, Sig Unander, the state's treasurer, had thrown his hat into the governor's race. Meanwhile, incumbent Robert Holmes made clear he would attempt to keep the governor's chair. Imagine the tensions if not outright verbal competition as the three met for Board of Control meetings, with the two Republicans, Hatfield and Unander, gearing up for the May primary and the winner knowing he would probably face Holmes in the fall. It was a situation without parallel in Oregon politics, before or after 1958.

Hatfield had hesitated in 1957 when friends and political advisors encouraged him to run for governor. As early as his first days as secretary of state, rumors flew around that he would soon run for senator, but as 1957 wore on more talk of a run for governor surfaced. Still, Hatfield kept quiet about that possibility—until the end of the year. Then, in early January, Hatfield's fellow legislator from Marion County, Lee Ohmart, polled members of the state legislature to get their opinions about possible Hatfield and Unander candidacies. The outcome of the poll, Hatfield said later, changed his mind. The legislators clearly favored Hatfield: thirteen of fifteen senators and thirteen of nineteen representatives preferred Hatfield over Unander.

Even after the favorable report, Hatfield continued to drag his feet, but in mid-January he moved on track and announced his run for the governor's office. Over the next four months, if it seems possible, Hatfield was even more often on the road speaking to a variety of meetings, especially up and down the Willamette Valley from Eugene to Portland. Surprisingly, quite often he and his competitor Unander appeared on the same platform to speak for their points of view.

At the end of March, Hatfield outlined his stances in the run for governor. A candidate "must be free from special political obligations," he said, "to act in [an] unfettered manner for all people." A candidate must also "make known his financial backers." He must keep up with all duties assigned to the governor's office, and he must "make periodic visits to state institutions." On the other side, candidates must eschew "sloganeering" and "vote-bait," that is, empty and misleading pledges that were impossible promises meant to stir up "nothing more than sloganeering." Finally, Hatfield pointed to his accomplishments as secretary of state and service on the Board of Control as solid evidence of how much Oregonians could trust and rely on him.

In his run-up to the primary, Hatfield made several choices that enhanced his candidacy. One of these was the selection of energetic former governor Elmo Smith as his campaign manager. Bringing onboard the noted conservative Republican leader illustrated Hatfield's strategy to sell himself as a representative to all Republicans—and perhaps to a few crossover Democrats. He also reached out to large groups of specific voters via his several speeches before women's groups. Hatfield was obviously going full tilt in the days closing out his primary run.

In another move to gain more support, a series of Hatfield advertisements hit the newspapers in the days just before the election. Again, journalists had fun playing with Hatfield's name and youth: voters should vote for Hatfield, "Mark the best man!"; he would provide "A Marked improvement"; and "*Old* Problems Need a *New* Approach." All of these ads contained a spiffy photograph of the young, handsome candidate.

The strategies and tireless moves proved extraordinarily successful. In March, Hatfield garnered in an excess of 100,00 votes, more than 40,000 over Unander, and more than Unander and third-place finisher Warren Gill, a Lebanon state senator, received together. Hatfield's strong finish

Mark Hatfield and Antoinette Kuzmanich, 1957. The handsome young couple first met in 1952, became engaged in late 1957, and married in Portland on 8 July 1958. Image courtesy of Willamette University Archives and Special Collections.

in the primary buoyed Republican hopes, many of the party now thinking he might be able to defeat incumbent Governor Holmes in the fall general election.

During the previous months and stretching into the summer, reporters took time out from their political reporting to light up stories of Hatfield's engagement and coming marriage to Antoinette Kuzmanich. Beginning in late 1957, newspapers announced the engagement and news of the impending marriage in the next mid-summer. News reports of Hatfield's appearances in the first months of 1958 often included photographs of the couple, featuring Hatfield's handsomeness and Antoinette's sparkling prettiness. A few bits of humor sneaked into the stories. For example, one reporter wrote, "Mark Hatfield takes a wife, and 99 per cent of Oregon's unattached gals head for California."

The Hatfield-Kuzmanich marriage took place in mid-July in Portland's Hinson Memorial Baptist Church. An overflow crowd of more than a thousand jammed the church. Not only was the longtime Oregon political leader finally getting married, he was an evangelical Baptist and Antoinette was raised Catholic. The differences in religious backgrounds engendered more than a few comments. Catholics were upset that Antoinette would leave her church to marry a Protestant, and Baptists wondered how one of theirs could marry a Catholic. To their credit, Mark and Antoinette worked out the differences. Eventually four children, two boys and two girls, blessed the high-publicity couple.

Hatfield did not let up on his energetic campaigning after his primary win and stretching on to the fall general election. His strategies were twofold: he would point out his achievements as secretary of state and, conversely, note the lack of successes, even failures, in Governor Holmes's administration. The major focus was the economy. Hatfield promised he would work at an "economic regeneration" in the state; it would be his "principal concern of the campaign." In turn, he would point to the "uncertain fiscal policies" of the current administration, showing how, for example, its tax policies had created an "uneasiness of corporations in not knowing what taxes they would have to face." Oregon's economy was faltering in mid-1958, meaning that Hatfield's promises and criticisms focused on the major challenge facing the state.

Just hours before the governor's race ended on 4 November, Senator Wayne Morse made a fateful decision to besmirch Hatfield's reputation. Viewed through hindsight, both Republican and several Democratic leaders saw the attack as, in the long run, beneficial for Hatfield and detrimental for Holmes. Morse's attack boomeranged.

Appearing on Portland Channel 5 on the eve of the election, Morse resurrected the tragic story of the seventeen-year-old Hatfield's traffic accident in which his car struck and killed a little girl just south of Salem. Reading the court records, Morse was convinced that Hatfield had lied about the case, covering up what had really happened. Coming to that conclusion and realizing that Holmes might be in need of last-minute help, the maverick Morse decided to attack Hatfield's credibility. As he told one listener, "I don't let a man run for public office who lies to a jury. I don't intend to let a man lie to a jury and get away with it." Others fired back, privately or publicly. One Democratic leader called Morse's TV talk "ill-timed, ill-tempered, and stupid." Other Democrats such as Edith Green, Charles O. Porter, and Richard Neuberger publicly "deplored" or "regretted" Morse's accusations. Morse himself did not answer the criticisms, but even his biographer Mason Drukman wondered if Morse wished, privately, that he had not launched the attack. A thick file in the Morse Papers at the University of Oregon Library reveals that dozens—maybe hundreds—of Oregon voters wrote to the senator denouncing Morse's harpooning of Hatfield.

As the fall campaign moved to its end, Holmes supporters were increasingly worried that the governor would be unable to defeat the surging Hatfield. Their worries were well founded. Even though Holmes was the incumbent and registered Democrats outnumbered Republicans in Oregon by 53,000, Hatfield galloped to a win. On 4 November, Hatfield won the election, garnering 331,900 votes to Holmes's 267,934, or a 55.3 to 44.7 percent victory.

Hatfield's sprint to the highest office in Oregon was nothing short of spectacular. In eight short years, he had quickly moved from a beginning state legislator with no previous public political experience to the chief executive's office. The magic of Mark had propelled him from his entry-level debut to Oregon's political apex in less than a decade. The youngest governor in the history of the state was now ready to take charge.

3

Oregon Governor, First Term, 1959–1963

Mark Hatfield's first years as governor soon revealed how much he had learned as a political leader in the previous eight years and how much he might need to comprehend in the next eight. His stint in the chief executive's office proved to be an in-between experience: building on his legislative and secretary of state time and preparing for the much longer thirty years in the U.S. Senate. The stay in the governor's chair proved to be the third stop in his four-stage political career: legislature, secretary of state, governor, and senator.

Over time, Hatfield told varied stories about the first months of his governorship. In his first book, *Not Quite So Simple* (1968), he reiterated his campaign pledges in describing his first chief executive activities. The Oregon economy was in shambles, he asserted, so he worked on that need. He also set out to make his office more efficient to keep down costs. Closely related was the need for more revenue; he went after new industries and businesses to add to the state's revenues. Hatfield also emphasized the necessity of reorganizing administrative agencies, cutting down on excessive numbers of committees and other organizations. He set out, too, to revise and clarify the state's cumbersome constitution.

Hatfield as governor. When Mark Hatfield became governor in 1959, he was the youngest chief executive in the history of the state. He would also become the first two-term Oregon governor in the twentieth century. State of Oregon *Official Voter's Pamphlet*, 1956, p. 71, and Oregon Historical Society, OrHi 83427.

Later in his final book, the memoir *Against the Grain: Reflections of a Rebel Republican* (2000), Hatfield told other stories. Rather than the economic needs and administrative reorganization mentioned more than twenty years earlier, he now pointed to *moral* questions as his most pressing and even traumatic issues. Most traumatic of all, he had to face moving ahead with executions—"Inheriting the Doomed"—because that was the Oregon law, even though he opposed capital punishment. In addition, he had to deal with the question of abortion and freedom-of-choice issues, although he wanted to avoid those controversies.

Some might make much of the difference of stories in the two books. Instead, they should realize that these were all front-and-center issues Hatfield had to face—ones throughout his political and personal careers. By dealing with both sets of controversies, Hatfield furnished a larger picture of the challenges lying before him as a new governor, albeit in two different versions.

Even before Hatfield officially became governor, a squabble broke out that disrupted Oregon's political scene. Both Hatfield and defeated but still governor Robert Holmes wanted to name the person to fill the remaining years of Hatfield's position of secretary of state. The political motivations of both leaders were understandable; having the secretary of state from their party—Hatfield (Republican), Holmes (Democrat)—meant keeping control of the three-person Board of Control and having a major ally in administering Oregon. Holmes, arguing he was still governor, named a replacement for Hatfield; but Hatfield asserted that he was still secretary of state until he took the governor's chair, and then once chief executive he would name his own replacement. Legal opinions flew as fast and furious as daily headlines—until the Oregon Supreme Court unanimously sided with Hatfield. Hours after he became governor, Hatfield named inexperienced but fellow Republican Howell Appling Jr. to be secretary of state.

Hatfield, just five weeks after winning the governorship and before he was officially sworn in as governor, showed another side of his personality that quickly enlarged his political notoriety in the next few years. He sent telegrams to six U.S. senators urging their support for more liberal Republican leadership in the Senate. His exhortations were meant to help them revitalize and recapture American political leadership by supporting "a vigorous, imaginative, progressive, alert Republican Party." Not satisfied to govern only in his own state, Hatfield was now reaching out to influence and even to lead nationally. These growing ties to national events expanded even farther when Hatfield hosted Vice President Richard Nixon to help celebrate the Oregon centennial. Those hectic hosting days were the beginnings of important links between Nixon and Hatfield that stretched on for more than a decade—before they turned in another direction.

Throughout his first term as governor, Hatfield followed most of his previous convictions about leadership and policymaking. Early in his political career, he became persuaded that rarely did a legislature, or voters, support a measure in its first introduction—sometimes not even in a reintroduction. Often a bill or petition had to be introduced three or four times before it won support from a legislature or voters. That being the case, more than a decade into his political career, Hatfield frequently put forth a favorite idea several times before it won support—or was finally rejected.

On 12 January 1959, Hatfield delivered his first inaugural address as governor. In his speech before the legislative assembly, he outlined a program that echoed much of what he had promised in his campaign against Governor Holmes. It was a comprehensive plan dealing with a better organized and more efficient government, reorganization of executive boards and committees, legislative procedures, revenues and taxation, expenditures, election reforms, and several other areas.

The subjects that immediately captured the most attention and divided Republicans and Democrats in the coming weeks were budget and taxation. Because Oregon had the highest income tax rate in the country, Hatfield needed to focus on that subject. He had done so in his campaigning for governor and now in his inaugural address. In the first weeks after Hatfield became governor and began to push his taxation measures, the issue turned rancorous. Not surprisingly, the reactions were extremely partisan. The senate president, Democrat Walter Pearson, was particularly negative in his comments on Hatfield's leadership in dealing with taxation policies. Hatfield's maiden speech, Pearson asserted, was "full of platitudes and well intentioned remarks, many of which didn't have much meaning." Monroe Sweetland, the Democratic senator from Milwaukie, pointed to what he considered Hatfield's misguided taxation guidelines. For Sweetland, Hatfield "advocated a Spartan tax policy which would eat the heart out of his advocacies before they could even get under way."

Republicans were much more positive. Robert Elfstrom, Republican leader in the Oregon house, praised Hatfield's "intention to steer the 'ship of state' on a true course of fiscal responsibility and maximum value received from each tax dollar." Republican senate floor leader Anthony Yturri was even more supportive. Hatfield's inaugural speech "was one of the most comprehensive addresses of its kind," showing an "unusual understanding of state problems and functions."

The election of 1958 had awarded Hatfield a Democratic state legislature. For the first time in the twentieth century—indeed, for the first time in nearly eighty years— the Democrats controlled both the senate and house. The senate had nineteen Democrats and eleven Republicans, the house thirty-three Democrats and twenty-seven Republicans. In the opening weeks of Hatfield's administration and the legislature's meetings, political jockeying was in full sway. A further challenge lay in two competing budgets: the earlier one introduced by defeated Governor Holmes and lying before the legislature, and the new one that Hatfield was gradually unrolling in January 1959. As conflicts between the executive and legislative branches began to emerge, Republicans asked the legislature to hold off in making large decisions on tax bills before Governor Hatfield had submitted a full budget proposal. They asked for "fair play" until the governor's plans were on complete display. In the month following the beginning of the new governor's administration, the two parties fired a continual barrage of political shots.

Then, on Monday, 9 February, Hatfield announced his budget plans. War broke out immediately, with partisan battles reaching explosive levels the next day in the state's newspapers. Some papers devoted parts of several pages to the fallout bursting out from the budget controversies.

Hatfield proposed a budget of nearly $313 million, up from more than $298 million in Governor Holmes's final budget. Income taxes would increase nearly $10 million, and more than $14 million of the budget would be dedicated to construction programs in the next two years. Income taxes would increase slightly, and deductions for federal taxes paid would be eliminated. Tax rates, generally, were lowered, but the governor also called for a 1 percent tax on all income, minus business expenses. Anyone without business or medical expenses would pay the flat tax of 1 percent. Hatfield viewed these changes as broadening the tax base and stiff-arming a possible sales tax. Overall, Hatfield was asking for a $9 million raise in taxes.

Journalists easily captured the obvious partisan reactions to Hatfield's budget and tax numbers. "Republicans were laudatory, Democrats derogatory"—as one reporter put it. Hatfield's supporters argued that he was embracing reality, with his budget figures fitting the future. Republican senator Donald Husband praised Hatfield's budget as "thoughtful and comprehensive" and lauded the governor's willingness to cut expenses. Conversely, Democratic house speaker Robert Duncan was a chief critic, depicting Hatfield as two-faced, "campaigning on a platform of economy" and now asking for more money and higher taxes. Democratic representative Keith Skelton agreed. He too thought Hatfield was guilty of double-speak, promising economies and savings and then calling for increased taxes and more spending. The partisan debate continued with Republican state chairman Peter Gunnar criticizing Democratic leader Pearson for not only failing to provide legislative leadership but also looking for ways to discredit Governor Hatfield.

Fortunately, not all was debate and controversy. Another sequence of events furnished respite from the political wars. On 14 February 1959, the state celebrated its centennial. Hatfield and his sparky wife Antoinette participated in several of the centennial festivities. The featured guest was Vice President Richard Nixon, who gave several presentations in a jam-packed, rain-drenched schedule. Most important, the vice president's trip fostered a closer friendship between Nixon and Hatfield. As Nixon prepared to fly back to Washington, D.C., he told a reporter that Hatfield was "one of the most outstanding young leaders the Republican Party has produced in recent years." Nixon added, "If Hatfield can make a good record as a governor," he clearly had "an important part to play with the Republican Party nationally." As if those encomiums were not enough, Nixon told the reporter that President Eisenhower had recently "spoke[n] very favorably of Hatfield." Taken together, these extraordinary positive comments from the country's two top Republicans must have buoyed Hatfield's spirits.

Another series of events provided separation from the party problems and hectic schedule of the centennial. The

Hatfields, once married and with him in the governor's office, began to look for a home in Salem. Both admired older homes and thus were drawn to a house at 883 S. High Street, part of which was ninety years old. Remodeling would include building a new section at the back of the house, digging a basement, and updating bathrooms. When furnished, the modest house would include 2,300 square feet of space. Over the years, the talented, energetic Mrs. Hatfield redecorated most of the house interior, cultivated surrounding garden spaces, and hosted hundreds—even thousands—of visitors.

Tensions between the Republican governor and the Democratic legislature continued into the spring. For example, Hatfield's tax plans engendered more opposition than support in the legislative branch. His push for lowering the voting age from twenty-one to eighteen also failed to gain Democratic backing. Even more disappointing for Hatfield was the Democratic opposition to his proposal to allow the governor to reorganize executive departments. Hatfield was especially "irked" when the house State and Federal Affairs Committee tabled the reorganization bill early in the legislative session. That decision, Hatfield predicted, "probably will be considered to be the worst decision it [the legislature] has made." Plus, Democrats were reluctant to speak for Hatfield's plan to launch a cigarette tax to fund a building program and instead spoke for a new sales tax, which the governor opposed. On several occasions, Democrats vowed to make Hatfield keep his campaign and inaugural promises of no new taxes, pointing out that he indeed was pushing for new sales taxes on cigarettes and gasoline. Democratic U.S. senator Richard Neuberger was especially direct, stating that Hatfield had "glibly promised voters lower taxes and a smaller budget" but had broken his promises by advocating new and added taxes. In more than one instance Hatfield, frustrated with Democratic opposition and negative votes, threatened to veto bills the Democrats wanted to

The Mark and Antoinette Hatfield home in Salem served as the governor's "mansion" during Hatfield's eight years as governor (1959–1967). The Hatfields renovated and enlarged the house. Author's photo.

pass. These threats drew the ire of more than a few Democrats. One resident writing a letter to the editor called Hatfield's threats acts of "political intrigue," acts that the letter writer had wished to avoid when he had immigrated to the United States.

Hoping to win more support in an increasingly Democratic state, Hatfield fostered compromises on divisive issues. Some revolved around laborers and labor unions. He called workers and businesses into his office to work out differences. Some negotiations worked, others not. Hatfield gained favor for his work on repealing an antipicketing law, but explosive divisions among loggers and log truck drivers and other labor groups destroyed nearly all détente between the governor and labor. One month after the legislature closed shop in early May, state labor leaders scored Hatfield's wrongheaded moves on legislation favorable to workers. In a letter to the governor, spokesmen for the AFL-CIO noted that, of Hatfield's more than fifteen vetoes, nine were on legislation on "which labor had either introduced or strongly supported."

Other Hatfield actions were much less controversial, in fact some gaining clear support. The governor's strong backing for improved race relations and civil rights, for example, elicited positive reactions. In a speech before the Portland Urban League on 26 April, Hatfield encouraged the four hundred members of his audience to urge legislators to pass bills now before the senate and house that included equality of housing and public accommodations. "Accelerate your actions," he told the listeners; do not let the measures get lost in the hectic last days of the legislative session.

But the central, always-on-the-docket issues in the legislature were those dealing with taxation, budgets, and needed revenues. During the 115 days of the Salem session, Republicans and Democrats were in nonstop contention, parrying one another and even stymied by tussles within each party. The major conflicts were over what and how taxes were to be levied. Democrats were unwilling to accept Hatfield's ideas of a base, 1 percent tax on all wages/income, widening the tax base, and a cigarette tax. Instead, some but not all Democrats pushed for a 3 percent sales tax that would largely fulfill revenue needs for escalating state costs. The state's most important newspaper, the Portland *Oregonian,* backed most of Hatfield's stances on taxation and revenue enhancement and criticized the Democrats for their "Flip-Flop-Flob" in handling tax programs. The Democrats, according to the newspaper editor, had "advanced, withdrawn, amended, compromised and rewritten in both houses and in conference committees" far too many measures. Their work was "a disgraceful end to a floundering session."

The *Oregonian* was dead center in its criticisms. The tax policies of the Democrat-driven legislature were muddled and unrealistic. Some of the Democratic-engineered bills Hatfield signed, others he vetoed. Of the seven hundred bills passed in the session, the governor signed a large majority, but he vetoed a total of seventeen, which he claimed as a new high in vetoes.

Other events during the nearly four-month long legislative session allowed for breaks from the political wrangling dominating Salem. These occurrences also furthered Hatfield's rapidly growing national notice. While on a trip to Washington, D.C., in mid-March, Hatfield spent time with Vice President Nixon and also met for forty-five minutes with President Eisenhower. Part of his agenda was to encourage the chief executive to add federal funding for the improvement of the Yaquina Bay Harbor and completion of the Green Peter Dam on the South Santiam River. The president did not respond to these requests but did surprise the young Oregon governor by quoting a line from Hatfield's inaugural address: "Is this essential or merely desirable; and, if it is only desirable, can I afford it?"

Another illustration of Hatfield's expanding notoriety was the essay "Oregon's Golden Boy," which appeared in the 9 May issue of the *Saturday Evening Post*. Washington, D.C.–based journalist Milton MacKaye provided a lively, appealing minibiography of Hatfield from his Dallas origins through his first months as governor. The author speculated that Hatfield and Nelson Rockefeller, rumored to be a Republican presidential candidate in 1960, "might make appealing running mates." MacKaye also noted Hatfield's close acquaintance with Billy Graham, who had stated recently, "I predict that if Mark Hatfield stays humble before the Lord, he will hold positions of national authority."

In the days and weeks immediately after the legislature closed its doors, Hatfield received more than a few comments about his leadership as a governor. Most of the journalists in the state saluted his executive work, none more than the *Register-Guard* in Eugene. The *Guard* hailed Hatfield as "doing a mighty fine job." Hatfield was "energetic and not playing it safe" and carrying out "a direct role in legislation." The governor had offered a "superb budget" and showed "a direct knowledge of his job . . . surrounded with skilled professionals." Portland and Salem newspapers were also supportive of Hatfield's first months of work. Later in the summer, however, some of his Democratic foes launched darts of criticism.

Once the tensions and challenges of the legislative session were over in early May, Hatfield was free to travel and make several delayed speeches. The trips included a five-day jaunt to the East, with nearly ten stops. While in New York City, he addressed the Christian Business Men's group and spoke to Republican groups in New York and Connecticut. He also spoke at Lafayette College and Houghton College, receiving honorary doctorates at both colleges. He was also a featured guest on Dave Garroway's *Today* TV show. Perhaps the most newsworthy of Hatfield's presentations was preaching in the pulpit of Norman Vincent Peale's Marble Collegiate Church in New York City.

The trip east and another to Puerto Rico to attend a national governors' gathering triggered more rumors and conversations about Hatfield's escalating rise in national politics. Later in the summer, he had a chat with Nelson Rockefeller, the newly elected governor of New York. The speculations about Hatfield's future usually focused on his being the vice-presidential candidate for Richard Nixon or Rockefeller in 1960. Most thought of Nixon as the leading presidential candidate and that Hatfield's temperament, political positions, and geographical location would fit more comfortably with Rockefeller than Nixon. And if Rockefeller could not, in turn, accept the vice-presidential nomination, "who," asked an *Oregonian* editorial, "would have more appeal than Hatfield?"

The series of events that captured most of Hatfield's time and energy was the Oregon centennial. From the beginning to the end of the summer, Oregon was awash in centennial events and extravaganzas. Hatfield spoke at several of these, dressed up for others, and marched in the parades of still others, especially on the western side of the state. It was also during the centennial that Hatfield made several contacts with Native American groups who participated in or were honored at these celebrations. These early contacts with Indian groups opened a career-long warm feeling between Native groups and the Oregon politician.

Still, not all was upbeat celebration and presentation for the governor in the summer of 1959. When either the governor or his legislative opponents mentioned what they considered the shortcomings of decisions in the 1959 winter and spring legislative sessions, those comments usually engendered spirited rebuttal from either side and sometimes from a third group. In mid-June, Democratic state senator Keith Skelton accused Hatfield of "attempting to intimidate" the legislature by refusing to sign or vetoing legislation that committees had set up to handle fiscal details. In response, Hatfield stated the bills were "unnecessary." Differences on tax policies dominated most of the exchanges. Hatfield pointed out that during the past legislative session the Democrats could not "get together on a tax program that I recommended," and that that failure resulted in fiscal challenges now facing the state. Democratic leader Ward Cook fired back that Hatfield was guilty of two mistakes: (1) the Democrats had put together a satisfactory tax program; it just did not follow Hatfield's desired guidelines; and (2) Hatfield's tax plan would have imposed an unpopular and unacceptable tax on "gross means of all persons before exemptions or deductions." At the same time, worker groups and skeptics were unhappy with the governor's labor policies and religious emphases and let the public often know of their discontent.

A notable event changed Hatfield's personal life in summer 1959, the birth of his first child, Elizabeth. Born to Antoinette on 2 July, the new daughter was named after the mother's cousin. Ten days before his thirty-seventh birthday, Hatfield had become a father. During the next two months, the Hatfields worked around their new needs at home but still attended many public events. News—and pictures—of the little addition to the Hatfield family often appeared in the pages of Oregon newspapers.

Hatfield's executive schedule in the fall seemed less hectic, but new controversies and tensions arose. The centennial shuttered its gates in mid-September, freeing the governor from many celebrity appearances and allowing other speech making. New clashes revolved around political and policy differences, especially as they involved Hatfield, Senator Richard Neuberger, and Congressman Charles O. Porter. Despite all these public presentations and appearances, the private life of the governor was not lost in the final months of 1959.

Hatfield's political activities followed state and national paths. The most widely covered Oregon controversy dealt with attempts to establish an Oregon Dunes state park or recreational area. Senator Neuberger, convinced that setting aside the Oregon coastal area stretching south of Florence was environmentally sound, became the most outspoken advocate of this endeavor. On several occasions he urged Hatfield to come onboard, declaring that if the governor did not support the Dunes park it would not come into existence. After several Neuberger urgings, Hatfield rather lamely indicated that he could not support the senator's bill but looked forward to more consideration of the idea. Congressman Porter furnished a second bill for the Dunes park in the House of Representatives, and he was even more explicit in calling for the governor's support of his legislation. Throughout the fall months, Neuberger and Porter tried to engage Hatfield in a conversation on the possible park.

Hatfield never made clear, publicly, his opposition to the Neuberger-Porter legislation. Was the governor agreeing with U.S. senators and representatives (Congress did not pass the Neuberger and Porter bills) who would not support the Dunes park because they thought it would be locking up natural resources? Or did he support coastal residents who were convinced that the recreation area would hurt them economically? Hatfield did not say. For more than a decade, moves for the Dunes park failed, until Hatfield's friend Republican congressman John Dellenbach introduced and successfully pushed through Congress legislation to establish the Oregon Dunes National Recreational Area in 1972.

In summer and fall 1959, media sources in Oregon were frequently capitalizing on Hatfield's quick rise as a national political figure. Nixon's visit to Oregon encouraged speculation about Hatfield's political future; so did Nelson Rockefeller's fall trip to the state. When the New York governor arrived in Oregon, he told a Eugene audience that Hatfield "would be a wonderful vice presidential candidate." Two days later Hatfield was in New York City and mentioned that, although Nixon was the obvious leading presidential candidate, in Oregon "it was a different story," suggesting that Rockefeller had pushed by Nixon as the Oregon favorite. In the weeks leading up to the holidays, Oregon newspapers continued touting Hatfield as a possible vice-presidential running mate, particularly for a Rockefeller presidential bid.

With the legislature out of session, fewer political clashes surfaced, but several differences of opinion on policy and political issues were clear enough. When the sprawling Harvey Aluminum Company at The Dalles tried to keep its tax assessment at $20 million rather than the $40 million backed by the Oregon Tax Commission, Hatfield weighed in on the commission side even though the large company threatened to kill a large planned expansion if the tax assessment was doubled. Hatfield also lobbied for a regional water and electric consortium rather than the other competing local and national positions on the touchy issue. The governor followed the same kind of middle-of-the-road policy dealing with several conservation measures, stating that they should be "carried on by both private and public agencies."

As the first year of Hatfield's gubernatorial leadership came to a close, pundits singled out a few of his achievements, ideas, and actions for special mention. Journalist Al McCready pointed to Hatfield's "national recognition" as a political newcomer and his strengths as a possible vice-presidential candidate of note. Another journalist emphasized that national political attention beginning to focus on Oregon in 1959 came about because Hatfield was such a "comer"; he had "won recognition as an outstanding GOP officeholder." Interestingly, Hatfield himself listed "government recognition, tax cutting and leadership in economic recovery" as his "major achievements."

Even in the midst of saluting Hatfield's political actions and achievements, writers did not overlook a few segments of his personal life. Antoinette Hatfield was praised as a first-rate hostess, and photos of months-old daughter Elizabeth graced some newspaper pages. Nor did journalists overlook the refurbished older house the Hatfields moved into in late November. One writer, on Christmas day, had the temerity to question whether Hatfield child "Number 2" was on the way. Hatfield would neither confirm nor deny the story.

In the opening weeks of 1960, Hatfield fulfilled his promise of going east to sell Oregon to prospective businesses. He also, directly or indirectly, expanded his own reputation as a promising political figure. Central to Hatfield's sales agenda for Oregon was his emphasis on the state's "livability," a theme he would promote for years to come. Attractive physical settings, mild climate, ambitious residents, and economic promise were key parts to Hatfield's livability agenda. He pointed to the Columbia River areas, including an area proximate to Boardman, and other possible government-owned areas as inviting possibilities for business expansion.

On these and other trips selling Oregon, Hatfield also burnished his promise as a young, arising Republican politician. He made new contacts and several speaking engagements. Talk continued about his possibility as a vice-presidential candidate, but a new rumor also surfaced suggesting that Hatfield might deliver the nomination speech for Richard Nixon at the next summer's Republican national convention.

Even more unusual notice of Hatfield came early in February 1960 with his autobiographical essay in Pastor Norman Vincent Peale's widely circulated magazine *Guideposts*. The piece was what evangelicals call a "testimony." Hatfield concisely summarized his life up to date, emphasizing the tenacity of his grandmother and mother for family and education and also stressing their "commitment." He had found their commitments bright lights for his own political career. More surprising, Hatfield spoke of his own recommitment as an adult in his late twenties to the teachings of Jesus Christ and to a life epitomizing those teachings. The *Oregonian* reprinted the essay—twice.

Although Hatfield hesitated to criticize his opponents, Democrats found several areas in which to harpoon the governor. The harshest of the critics was Democratic state chairman Robert Straub, who accused the governor of favoring the sterilization of unwed mothers via state welfare aid. Straub's charge was wrong—or at least misleading. The governor had accepted the controversial sterilization topic, along with several others, as worthy of discussion by the state public welfare commission, but he did not speak in support of the idea. Straub did not let up, wishing to brand Hatfield as an advocate of sterilization and holding secret meetings to discuss the idea. Other Democrats pilloried Hatfield for raising taxes, increasing the budget, and making false campaign promises. To most of these attacks Hatfield did not respond, although his staff members branded Straub a "liar" for accusing Hatfield of favoring sterilization.

Several unsettling challenges remained in early 1960. Although compromises on both sides had pushed a proposed Dunes park on the coast toward acceptance in Congress, that measure remained unfilled. Hatfield also had been unable to midwife the settlement of a labor strike that complicated the publication of two of the state's leading newspapers, the *Oregonian* and the *Oregon Journal*. Tax controversies continued to upset the state.

The largest new challenge came unexpectedly in the sudden death of Senator Neuberger and how he should be replaced in the U.S. Senate. A 1953 Oregon law, possibly unconstitutional, stated that the governor must appoint a person from the same party as that of the deceased. Hatfield added that he would not name the replacement from those who had already filed to run in the fall 1960 to replace Neuberger. That meant Maurine Neuberger, the late senator's widow, would not be named to complete her husband's

Senate term. After a good deal of hesitation, Hatfield named Democrat Hall S. Lusk, a seventy-six-year-old associate justice of the Oregon Supreme Court, to be Neuberger's replacement. Less than two weeks later, Hatfield traveled east to see Lusk sworn in at a Senate meeting and took the new senator to meet President Eisenhower.

As spring transitioned into summer, Hatfield found himself following more familiar than new tracks. He continued his never-stop schedule of speaking at political, church, educational, and women's gatherings. Reacting to these frequent talks, critics frequently denounced Hatfield for "politicking" when he should be governing. But they failed to see that the governor was doing what he had done since 1950 as a politician, taking his ideas and proposed actions to as many and as varied audiences as possible.

Several of the measures he spoke for were those he had announced and supported early in his governorship. He organized and encouraged a committee to look for ways to streamline the executive branch of Oregon government, particularly by instituting something of a cabinet organization that would report to the governor. He continued to push for advancement of Oregon industry, businesses, and tourism. Particularly of interest was developing the Boardman area of eastern Oregon near the Columbia River as something of a state-sponsored industrial park. Without any new information from the governor, news reports continued that Hatfield might run for the U.S. Senate against Wayne Morse in 1962.

In the midst of his sometimes nearly frenetic political schedule, Hatfield also made news in his personal life. He announced that, after encouragement from a New York publisher, he was beginning a book on U.S. governors (the book was never written). He also found time to pen an essay on his married life for *Coronet* magazine titled "We Kept the 'Obey' in Our Marriage." Even more surprising, eastern writer James Reichley produced a novel titled *Hail to the Chief* (1960), which obviously referenced Hatfield in speaking of his hero as a "handsome, young (38) governor of Oregon" with ambitious political aspirations. And on Sunday, 19 June, son Mark O. "MarkO" Hatfield Jr. was born to the Hatfields, a prime present on Father's Day to join a year-old sister.

Over time Hatfield was garnering numerous positive reports about his governing. Nearly every month the Portland *Oregonian* praised the governor's leadership, especially his tireless work to boost the state's economy, to enhance its livability, and to reach out to Oregonians generally. The Eugene *Register-Guard* was similarly upbeat, commending Hatfield and his staff for an outstanding job in "selling Oregon." The "sellers" had done so well, the *Guard* editorialized, "that several firms have indicated a real interest in coming to our state."

The high point for Hatfield in summer 1960 was his selection to introduce Vice President Nixon in his run for the presidency at the Republican national convention in Chicago. Most of all, Hatfield had hoped to deliver the keynote address just as the equally youthful Idaho senator Frank Church had done at the Democratic convention. Hatfield had even encouraged his selection as the Republican keynoter. But to his disappointment that did not happen.

It was clear now that Hatfield would not keynote the Republican gathering, but what his role at the convention would be remained mysterious. On 11 June, less than two months before the Republican gathering to nominate a presidential candidate, it was rumored that Hatfield could be given a place on the convention program "at least equal" to giving the keynote. Nothing more appeared in the press about the possible program participation. Six weeks later an unconfirmed report made the rounds in Portland that Hatfield would introduce Nixon. The report was confirmed on

22 July, less than a week before the introduction took place. Hatfield revealed that he was surprised to get the invitation from Nixon himself.

Hatfield promised a short speech. On the evening of Wednesday, 17 July, the thirty-eight-year-old Oregon governor nominated Richard Nixon for president in a speech of less than three minutes. In a presentation of 280 words that journalists praised for its precise diction, Hatfield saluted Nixon and his "awesome responsibility" and "courage in crisis." For Hatfield, Nixon had also "trod the path of peacemakers," but in doing so he had not surrendered "the hopes, the ambitions, the achievements of the nation." The nomination speech "lit the fuse of an explosion," with the enthusiastic Republicans on their feet and cheering for nearly twenty minutes after Hatfield's nomination.

Hatfield's position as Nixon's nominator contained conflicting surprises. On Hatfield's side, even before the convention he had clearly encouraged Nelson Rockefeller to allow his name to come up for presidential nomination. When Rockefeller chose not to, Hatfield pushed on to have Rocky chosen as Nixon's vice-presidential running mate. That push continued up to the beginning of the convention, even though by that time Hatfield had been selected as Nixon's nominator. On Nixon's side, surely he must have been surprised—and perhaps had second thoughts—when Hatfield continued to advocate so vociferously for Rockefeller's political future even after having been chosen to nominate Nixon. Neither side, however, spoke of these possible surprises. During the 1960s, Hatfield seemed to be a supporter of Nixon and even later was thought of as Nixon's choice for a vice president in 1968, but marked differences between the two western politicians would also emerge during these years.

Some Republican critics—and also a few Democrats— pilloried Hatfield for what they asserted was his unwillingness to identify as a Republican in his run for the governor's chair in 1958. That criticism, if at all convincing, proved groundless in the fall of 1960. After the presidential nominations in summer and as the November elections loomed, Hatfield launched a nearly endless series of presentations supporting Republican candidates in Oregon, other parts of the West, and even in some locations in the East.

Actually, Hatfield had been on the move since he was elected governor. In late September, the Salem *Oregon Statesman* reported that Hatfield had set a new travel record for Oregon governors. During his twenty and half months in office, he had traveled out of state for 113 days. Travis Cross, Hatfield's press secretary, stated that forty of these days were to make political presentations, the remainder for state duties. As the schedule ramped up moving toward November elections, Hatfield's time on the road expanded. As the *Oregonian* noted, Hatfield was "much in demand as a campaigner for Republican candidates on the national ticket and in others states." The Portland newspaper urged Oregonians not to think that Hatfield traveled too much—although Mrs. Hatfield might. Besides, bipartisan strength was expanding when Hatfield was out of Oregon: Walter Pearson, the Democratic senate president, was acting governor when Hatfield traveled. Throughout the early fall, Hatfield traveled to speak for western and Oregon Republican candidates. On one occasion in late October on a hectic plane and car trip, the governor spoke at Roseburg, Empire, Coos Bay and North Bend, Gold Beach, and Medford—all in one day.

Not surprisingly, in Oregon Hatfield spoke supportively of Nixon, vice-presidential candidate Henry Cabot Lodge, and other Republicans. In these presentations, Hatfield took a double-barreled approach: he would salute the stances of the candidates but also include support for his own views, as long as they were not counter to the ideas of the candidates. For instance, Hatfield could speak more as a follower of Herbert Hoover in emphasizing power at the state and local levels without undermining Nixon's need, as president, for strong central government.

During the course of 1960, Oregon attorney general Robert Y. Thornton and Hatfield were increasingly at odds. An outspoken Democrat, Thornton became Hatfield's major political antagonist in the fall. Thornton was understandably upset when the governor repeatedly chose to follow the advice of Loren Hicks, a lawyer and Hatfield's legal counselor, rather than the views of the attorney general in constitutional matters. Hatfield also accused Thornton of going slow on measures Hatfield promoted but the attorney general opposed. These mounting conflicts help to explain Thornton's attempt, two years later, to unseat Hatfield in the gubernatorial election of 1962.

The big story in fall 1960 should have been the presidential election in November. In some ways it was for Hatfield. Oregon voted for Hatfield's candidate, Richard Nixon, by 408,060 votes over John F. Kennedy's 367,402. But in the national outcome Kennedy narrowly pushed past Nixon by less than 120,000 out of more than 60 million votes. Nixon's win in Oregon was all the more remarkable since the state featured 75,000 more registered Democrats than Republicans.

As we have seen, Hatfield pressed hard for Nixon in the weeks before the election, but if he reacted privately to the disappointment of the vice president's defeat he did not speak publicly about the loss. In fact, just days after the election, Hatfield and his wife joined more than twenty U.S. governors for a fifteen-day trip to South America. The state leaders were responding to a South American invitation, probably launched as an attempt to increase U.S. state trade with neighbors to the south. In reacting to opponents' criticism of his being out of the state too often, Hatfield defended the trip as part of his large goal of expanding the Oregon economy. Whatever the purpose of the trip, the governor's being in South American countries lessened his commentary on the outcome of the 1960 election.

The issues that aroused the most comment in the closing days of 1960 were Hatfield's proposed budget and the program he planned to submit to the state legislature in early 1961. Hatfield introduced a budget asking for a 5 percent jump in total expenditures but no raise in taxes. In an editorial, the *Oregonian* supported Hatfield's proposed budget, calling it in all ways "reasonable."

If the planned budget stirred up little opposition, Hatfield's repeated call for government reorganization of the state's executive branch generated opposition—and quickly. In his nearly two years as governor, Hatfield viewed the multiple, diverse groups in charge of many Oregon activities as too separate, disorganized, and difficult for an executive to administer. To solve this situation, in mid-December Hatfield called for a cabinet-like administration of "seven new state departments, the director of each to be appointed by the governor and confirmed by the state senate." The new departments would deal with social services, transportation and utilities, public safety, natural resources, labor, commerce, and revenue. The Department of Education would remain, but the Board of Control would be eliminated.

Obviously, Hatfield was outlining a plan that would greatly increase the governor's appointment powers. Rather than emphasize that shift, Hatfield stressed that the changes would "make executive agencies more responsive to the will of the people and would permit improved coordinations, greater economy and more effective services."

Opponents thought differently. They wondered about so much new power in the governor's hands, especially Democrats who thought Hatfield was bent on empowering his own career. Labor leaders spoke against the proposed changes, chiefly the change that would take leadership decisions out of their hands and give them to the governor.

Even Secretary of State Howell Appling Jr. (a Hatfield appointee) and State Treasurer Howard Belton (also a Hatfield appointee), Hatfield's colleagues on the three-man Board of Control, spoke out against the proposed closing of the board. They were more convinced than Hatfield that the board, not scattered groups, was the best central place for their administrative decisions. Others expressed their disagreement with Hatfield's government reorganizational plans but decided to wait until the 1961 Oregon legislature to express their opposition.

As 1960 moved to a close, Hatfield had obviously gained a majority of supportive Oregon voters. Those backers particularly were drawn to Hatfield's energy and enthusiasm, his commitment to fiscal responsibility, and his championing of their state. Still, others had reservations about the governor's reorganizational plans, his traveling so often out of state, and his tendency to throw too much at one time at legislators and voters. This combination of support and opposition faced Hatfield when the new year and new legislature of 1961 stood before the governor.

As 1961 opened, there was clear evidence of Republican resurgence in Oregon. The Republicans had bounced back from a low point politically in the mid-1950s. Hatfield advocates frequently pointed to the governor's strong leadership and popularity as the major reason for this Republican turnaround. Building on that sensed resurgence, Hatfield was laying out expansive plans for the next year.

On Monday, 9 January 1961, in his state of the state address to the Fifty-First Oregon State Legislative Assembly, Hatfield reiterated several ideas that he had pushed for since becoming governor two years earlier. At the top of the list was his ambitious, often-repeated plan to reorganize the executive branch of the Oregon government. He would also continue to support a more equitable tax system by widening the tax base and holding the line against overall higher taxes. For senior citizens, he urged implementation of a health insurance plan for the elderly and a homestead exemption from property tax. And, as he would state about six years later in *Not Quite So Simple,* "the most serious problem" he faced as governor "was the economic deterioration of Oregon and the loss of employment opportunities." He would try to urge the legislature in 1961 to address these problems.

The fifty-first legislature opened in Salem on 9 January and lasted until 11 May, a 122-day session, the second longest to that time in Oregon history. Hatfield quickly introduced his large, ambitious plan to reorganize the executive branch of the state government. He was convinced that the reorganization would bring increased efficiency, lower costs, and more control to an unwieldy system. His plans for reorganization were extraordinarily detailed.

Once introduced, the Hatfield plan for reorganization drew immediate reactions—most of them negative. In a Democratic-dominated legislature (thirty-one to twenty-nine in the house, and twenty to ten in the senate), there was a good deal of opposition to Hatfield's call for reorganization. The opponents said the revisions would give too much power to the Republican Hatfield and take away leadership from strong, helpful committee and board executives. Democratic senate president Harry D. Boivin revealed that he was "not enthusiastic" about Hatfield's suggested cabinet reorganization plan. Senator Alfred H. Corbett, another Democrat, added that Hatfield's ideas and actions were clear evidence of his "taking over the reins of power." The Medford *Mail Tribune,* labeling Hatfield "a determined young man, and an aggressive one," criticized the governor's reorganization plans as a "grab for power."

Hatfield, of course, disagreed. He was not trying to "grab power," he asserted, but attempting to streamline executive leadership and actions for the good of the state. As the legislature progressed from January to May, the opposition to executive reorganization mounted. Seeing the difficulty before them, Hatfield and his supporters decided to break down the larger plan into several separate bills. That did not work either. By the end of the session, nearly twenty-five separate bills harboring parts of the larger reorganization plan were voted down or tabled. One of the most important of these was the failure of Hatfield to gain his desired end of the Board of Control and the reassignment of many of its decisions to the governor's office. After the defeat of Hatfield's reorganizational efforts, the legislature, as a sop in the governor's direction, allocated $100,000 to his office so that he could hire four new assistants to aid him in his executive duties and actions.

The defeat of Hatfield's much-desired reorganization must have been very disappointing to the young governor. If so, he did not speak extensively about his disappointment. He did admit a bit later, however, that perhaps "we asked for too big a change all at once." He thought, too, that maybe he misunderstood how most Oregonians felt. They were convinced that "it's gone along pretty well the way it's been. Why change?"

In another way, Hatfield may have, in his own actions, undercut support for his reorganization plans. In the third year of his governorship an event complicated his efforts. When the welfare commission opposed some of the governor's ideas and failed to act quickly on his requests, the chief executive requested that four members of the commission, which he had not appointed, resign. It was a disturbing request and played into the hands of his foes. Opponents of reorganization now had evidence, they were convinced, of the governor's intention to grab power. Hatfield countered these views, but his urging the welfare commission members to resign revealed, his critics asserted, what would happen if Hatfield's reorganization plan was passed in the legislature, giving much more appointment power to governors. The upset surrounding the welfare commission on the eve of legislative decisions in early 1961 played against, not for, Hatfield. He chose not to speak or write later about the controversies surrounding the welfare commission.

Although Hatfield spoke about Oregon's economic needs as his most important challenge as governor, he was not as active in this area of need in the legislative period of 1961 as he had been in 1959. He did push for several actions, however. Chief among these was the ongoing series of steps to transform lands near Boardman into a space-age developed area. The navy was already using the area, but now in a series of agreements between Washington, D.C., and Salem the area was nearly ready for the Boeing company to take over and develop a large tract of land for rockets and missiles. Whether the land would be purchased outright or involved in a trade between federal- and state-owned lands was still to be decided. Also, Hatfield encouraged Oregonians residing close to Tongue Point on the Columbia near Astoria to help ready that area for economic development. The governor likewise delighted in luring the International Paper company of New York into building a large pulp and paper mill near Gardner on the Oregon coast.

Some of these expansions, as well as other decisions, pushed Hatfield into environmental issues. Firms already at Boardman, and others wishing to launch a business there, wanted access to the Columbia. How was protection of the river water to be worked out? International Paper wished to dump effluent into the Pacific. How was that possible pollution to be handled? Loggers and lumbering firms wanted to cut more trees to capitalize on Oregon's timber riches. Hatfield began to work on that production-conservation issue as a middle-of-the-roader, a position that upset born-again environmentalists, especially Democratic environmentalists, in Hatfield's later senator years. Finally, he also looked carefully at dams and other water decisions so as to avoid endangering salmon runs. Whether Governor Hatfield saw himself as a conservationist or environmentalist is

not entirely clear (although later he claimed to be environmentally conscious), but he obviously was forced to make
decisions in these controversial areas in the early months
of 1961.

Hatfield was also bent on keeping at and bringing to
Salem several state agencies. He wanted those organizations to be close at hand because he was convinced that
proximity augmented smooth, more expeditious working
order. The most contentious of his actions was deciding to
move the state welfare department from Portland to Salem.
About half of the two hundred or so employees in the
department rejected the executive order by resigning and
looking for other employment. These disgruntled workers
wanted to avoid disrupting their families and having to sell
their homes. A handful of "Negro employees" would not
move to Salem "because of the unwelcome climate toward
Negroes in the state capital." Not so, Hatfield replied; several African American employees in Salem reported "they
are well received in their neighborhoods." Legislative members were sufficiently upset with Hatfield's executive decision that they introduced a bill to counter his action. The
bill passed both houses, but the governor vetoed the measure. The legislative votes were not sufficient in number to
override his veto; his executive order remained in effect, and
the welfare department moved to Salem.

Ironically, even though several of Hatfield's most-desired
measures failed to pass the legislature, the young governor
remained eminently popular in the state. Rumors surfaced
periodically that he would run against Wayne Morse for the
U.S. Senate in 1962. A group in California even spoke of
Hatfield as a presidential candidate in 1964, particularly
since Californian Richard Nixon chose not to be a candidate. Undoubtedly Hatfield's energetic work as governor,
as speaker, as participant in a multitude of public gatherings
and celebrations, and his rather muted responses to fiery
opposition helped keep him popular in Oregon. Nor should

one overlook the value of Antoinette Hatfield's partnership as hostess, food preparer, and sometimes presenter. On several occasions during the legislative weeks, legislators and their spouses were invited to visit and chat at the Hatfields' refurbished home in Salem. When photographers pictured the Hatfields, their youthfulness, smiles, and Antoinette's bright eyes dominated the photographs.

But the never-stop work during the legislative term took its toll on the governor. In the middle of the session, he was taken to the hospital and stayed there nearly a week. Exhaustion was a major reason for the hospitalization. Hatfield promised to cut back on his schedule, especially his numerous speeches at all kinds of meetings, but newspapers reported that he was still speaking several times each week.

When the legislative session ended in early May, Hatfield was disappointed, generally, with the outcome. He saw the legislature as "marked by bitter struggles." The divisions within the Republican and Democratic parties, as well as between them, and among the legislators themselves were major barriers to achieving more. He was, of course, frustrated that his reorganization dreams "fared so poorly." Nor had the legislators given much-needed tax relief to the elderly or enacted his traffic safety measures. Still, there were the achievements at Boardman, International Paper's move into the state, and helpful decisions on taxes and his budget.

Oregonian reporters were of another view. They saw the legislative session as "much more positive." It ended with "good feelings," and overall it was a "'plus' legislature." True, rifts in the two parties kept the session from achieving much more, the newspaper admitted, but, "in total, the 1961 Assembly was more constructive than otherwise." Oregon voters should be satisfied with what happened in Salem because the "state was in pretty good shape."

As was usually the case in an Oregon legislative year, political activities slowed down considerably in 1961 after the end of the Salem session. In the nearly eight months after the close, Mark Hatfield kept at his usual hectic pace, but his actions and activities differed markedly from those in the first four months of the year.

First, the governor had to deal with legislative leftovers. Chief of these was signing or vetoing bills the state house and senate had passed. More than seven hundred bills were passed in the busy legislature, and Hatfield signed nearly all of them, vetoing about twenty. One of the most controversial vetoes was the governor's putting the kibosh on the bill to keep the state's welfare commission in Portland rather than transferring it to Salem, which Hatfield had done through executive order.

The controversies between the governor and the welfare commission raced on. But later in 1961, through his executive power, Hatfield appointed new commission members amenable to residing in Salem and to following his tight budgets for a welfare system that threatened to fall deeply into the red. Of the 205 salaried positions, only 195 had been filled, and 107 had resigned rather than move to Salem. In clashes with the commission, Hatfield showed his Republican fiscal colors by maintaining a tight control on expenditures, keeping to available funds, and speaking against new, larger funding.

In commenting on his political views dealing with national and state issues, Hatfield tried to maintain a middle-of-the-road position. Speaking to the Oregon Republican Club in Portland in late September, he told the audience, "We should look for things the state can do better, but some things can be done better by the federal government." His fellow Republicans, Hatfield added, must maintain their attention to individual rights, but they must not overlook the needs of the less fortunate. These positions, part Republican/part Democratic in the early 1960s, revealed the moderate Republicanism of the energetic governor.

The shift from the Eisenhower to Kennedy presidency in 1961 led to less Hatfield involvement in national political affairs. The Hatfield fan club of President Eisenhower and Vice President Nixon disappeared from the White House, and the Democrats did not bring to their leadership anyone well connected to Hatfield. In fact, Hatfield said surprisingly little about national affairs in the second half of 1961. He might back Kennedy's criticism of communists and Russia, but he was less involved in other issues. Hatfield's focus was increasingly on state affairs.

As the months wore on in 1961, Oregon newspapers periodically predicted what Hatfield would do politically in 1962. Their predictions often conflicted with the paths Hatfield laid out and followed. Looking for a competitive Republican opponent for Senator Wayne Morse in his reelection bid, more than a few journalists frequently turned to Hatfield as the strongest, most logical candidate to compete with Morse. Hatfield, however, told readers and listeners throughout 1961 that he intended to run for reelection in 1962 and become the first two-term Oregon governor of the twentieth century.

Once political pundits accepted Hatfield's planned path, they turned to looking at possible competitors to run against the sitting governor. The first to announce his race against Hatfield was Robert Y. Thornton, a left-leaning Democrat, then in the middle of his fourth term as Oregon's attorney general. In late October, Thornton announced he would run against Hatfield because of the governor's wrongful actions on welfare issues, offshore oil drilling, and daylight-saving time. Hatfield had also been guilty, Thornton added, of a "misuse of power" by "devising stunts designed to produce a steady flow of publicity to glamorize Mr. Hatfield and elevate him to higher political office."

The other leading Democrat to jump into the governor's race was state senator Walter J. Pearson of Portland. An enthusiastic, outspoken conservative, Pearson announced his attempt to unseat Hatfield. The governor's record in office, Pearson declared, was rife with "misleading and broken campaign promises." Pearson particularly objected to what he saw as Hatfield's failure to support a workmen's compensation bill, lower property taxes, and a "realistic program for education." Pearson promised he would go after the governor with a "hard, fighting campaign."

Strangely, even though Hatfield frequently stated his intention to run for a second term as governor, several writers and political advocates began in the second half of 1961 to tout him as a possible candidate for the presidency in 1964. When Richard Nixon announced he would not run again for the White House in 1964 and instead threw his hat into California's gubernatorial race in 1962, the cheers for Hatfield grew even more frequent. In the June issue of *McCall's Magazine*, for example, Hatfield was listed as a "bright young man" worthy of greater political consideration. One Oregon journalist praised Hatfield as a "fresh, new face" for western Republicans. But Hatfield himself wobbled when questioned about presidential ambitions. In June, when asked about a run for the presidency at the national governors conference in Hawaii, he told a questioner, "I'm not actively seeking the nomination, but I'm not closing any doors." A few days later and back in Oregon, Hatfield dismissed presidential rumors as "just sea breeze." As the year progressed, political commentators moved away from Hatfield as presidential candidate to focus on his rerun for the governor's chair.

Several not-easily-solved issues occupied much of Hatfield's time from spring to late winter 1961. With some he failed; with others he had a modicum of success. When the legislature fumbled bills on daylight-saving time and rural and urban voters came to conflicting decisions on the emotional issue, Hatfield seemed to be waffling and sufficiently uninterested in pushing hard for a solution. He refused to call for a special session of the legislature to address the conflict and did not advance a possible answer to the dilemma. Similar delays characterized Hatfield's dealings with fallout shelters, which became a national and state issue in the cold war of the early 1960s. Hatfield constructed a fallout shelter in his own basement but failed to get Oregon political leaders behind his less-than-all-out support for the shelters.

Other Hatfield failures surfaced. His efforts to block convicts from working on government buildings hit a dead end when his two colleagues on the Board of Control—Secretary of State Appling and State Treasurer Belton—outvoted Hatfield and allowed contractors to use the convicts as laborers. Perhaps the numerous, dramatic conflicts surrounding state welfare policy were unsolvable, but Hatfield certainly was not successful in addressing these mammoth problems. The governor's largest defeat was his inability to get legislators to support his state executive reorganization plans or to gain sufficient voter backing to push through the ambitious proposal.

Hatfield's successes outweighed his failures, however. He completed negotiations to establish the Boardman and Boeing installation. He worked well with laborers and contractors in settling labor disputes, proving to be a superb mediator between fiery opponents, something that other Oregon Republican politicians could not achieve. In addition, he held the line on taxes, as he had promised. Plus, he energetically backed new community colleges in Oregon and worked smoothly with the new presidents of the University of Oregon and Oregon State University.

And was anyone in the entire state more energetic in "selling" Oregon? In addition to the previously mentioned expansions, Hatfield also enthusiastically promoted Oregon highways, often showing up to celebrate the openings of freeway sections or newly constructed state highways. Nor did the youthful governor back away from his energetic speech making even though his hectic schedule had endangered his health earlier in the year. His optimism was catching—and inspiring. When a writer for the *Saturday Evening Post* argued that Oregon was "in doldrums,"

Hatfield fired back, with evidence, that the writer was mistaken and misinformed.

Hatfield's own conclusions came at the end of the year. The *Oregonian* requested that the governor provide an overview of what he had accomplished in his three years as governor. It was an ideal outlet for Hatfield to list—even brag about—his achievements. His brief overview filled an entire page in the state's leading newspaper.

Hatfield pointed to several achievements in his role as the "people's lobbyist." His numerous appointments, including seventy-seven circuit court judges and numerous others, had worked well. These good appointees nearly always won reelection on their own. Overall, Hatfield believed, he had been a leader for the entire state and its varied interests. Numerous "cabinet" meetings, discussions of all sorts, and other mediations with laborers, welfare recipients, and medically challenged persons, Hatfield was convinced, were evidence of his broad-based leadership. The governor also listed achievements in educational, environmental, and taxation arenas as proofs of his successes.

Some of the accomplishments Hatfield enumerated were, in effect, answers to his opponents. True, welfare dilemmas were a challenge. But clear gains in that area were now apparent in new programs for the aged, in mental health, and for the medically challenged; these gains must not be overlooked. And the move of the welfare commission to Salem deserved credit for fostering closer and better working relations between the state's government and welfare needs. Hatfield was certain, too, that his support for education, natural resources, and economic development more than offset the criticisms of naysayers.

Hatfield ended his apologia with a salute to Oregon and its residents. An Oregonian was an "individualist," the governor opined; "he freely says what he thinks" and lives out the "heritage of the independent pioneer of a century ago."

Hatfield was "grateful" to be the leader of these green-loving, unique Oregonians.

Early in 1962, the major political events of the year were beginning to surface in Oregon and would remain onstage throughout the coming months. Democrats were eager to find ways to oust Hatfield from the governor's office. To do that, they harpooned his actions as chief executive and boasted of their own strengths as leaders. Hatfield's major Democratic opponents, as mentioned, were a state senator, Walter J. Pearson, and the attorney general, Robert Y. Thornton. They were the major harpooners of the governor.

Pearson, the more conservative of the Democratic duo, hurled several charges at Hatfield. First of all, the governor and University of Oregon president Arthur Fleming were wrong and did Oregonians a disservice by allowing communist Gus Hall to speak at the Eugene campus. Pearson also denounced Hatfield's "net receipts" tax, calling instead for a more equitable sales tax. Moreover, according to Pearson, Hatfield was muddling along on daylight-saving time issues. Seeking a valuable entry into the campaign, Pearson requested a debate with Hatfield, in which he would show Oregonians Hatfield's shortcomings in fiscal policies, revenue building, and his "double-talk."

For Pearson, Hatfield had been a weak leader. As the state senator put it, "The legislature should not be expected to lead the governor around by the hand." Scarcely more than a week later, Pearson lambasted Hatfield for "avoiding the truth on issues" and for being so uncooperative with "the present federal administration and the Oregon Legislature." Two months later after Thornton (149,000) pummeled Pearson (61,331) in the Democratic primary, the conservative antagonist withdrew into silence.

Attorney General Thornton, said by some journalists to be more liberal than Hatfield, launched a negative campaign against the governor. They had clashed on several issues previous to the campaign of 1962. In late January in his home county of Tillamook where he had served as city attorney, Thornton accused Hatfield of exorbitant spending, including for a "$13,000 a year state-paid political manager and strategist." Hatfield also had, Thornton continued, a "private attorney" at $13,000 plus and a limousine, and he made excessive, expensive trips out of state. Nearly two months later, Thornton attacked Hatfield's reorganization plan calling for the governor's appointment of the attorney general and secretary of state.

Hatfield did not respond to the sharp charges, but his administrative assistant Travis Cross did. Thornton was, Cross fired back, a "one-crack mind," and then a fusillade of Cross zappings followed. "Oregonians have become accustomed to . . . Thornton's loosely drawn opinions," Cross added, and these "indictments and investigations . . . have ended up in high costs, [and] precious few convictions." Finally, Cross noted that Thornton's many "finger-pointers simply can't be trusted."

But Thornton did not let up, especially with the May primary looming. In late March the attorney general jabbed Hatfield's removal of the state welfare department to Salem, asserting that the move reduced the amount of funds available for pressing welfare needs. That decision was "an abuse of power" and needlessly added to welfare expenditures. Just days before the 19 May primary, Thornton joined other Democratic candidates in showing their view that they did not "think much of the record of Gov. Mark O. Hatfield, a Republican." In the days after winning the Democratic primary, Thornton continued his criticisms of Hatfield. In the view of the *Oregonian* editorial page, Thornton's attack on the governor's uncertain position on daylight-saving time was not so much aimed at that issue itself but in "furthering his campaign to win the governorship." For Thornton, Hatfield had been and continued to be "unresponsive to the public will." Thornton's attacks on the governor would continue—and accelerate—in the next six months.

While Hatfield was suffering a barrage of negativity from Pearson and Thornton, he also faced other less-than-positive reactions. Maurine Neuberger challenged the governor to do something about her—and her husband's earlier—proposal to establish a national park in the Dunes area on the coast. Even more dispiriting was a political poll taken in the spring. In the Portland area nearly seven hundred voters in Multnomah, Clackamas, and Washington counties were asked to rank Hatfield's work as governor. About 39 percent gave him a "good" ranking and 33 percent "only fair." Only 9 percent evaluated Hatfield's actions as "excellent."

But other state and national reactions were much more positive. The Portland *Oregonian* was a bulwark of support. State political writer Merwin Shoemaker, in early January, predicted Hatfield would not have "significant primary opposition" in June. The newspaper's backing was even more explicit as the weeks wore on. In a lead editorial just before the primary election, a journalist stated baldly that Hatfield had "earned reelection by his progressive policies, his liberal approach to state problems and his courage in advocating programs in the best interests of the people." Two days later, the periodical endorsed Hatfield for reelection to the governor's chair.

Outsiders were also praising Hatfield. A national Gallup poll listed Hatfield as one of the ten leading Republican possible presidential candidates. Senator Barry Goldwater, at the opposite end of Hatfield's political stances, nonetheless applauded the governor's anticommunist statements. A visitor from Japan praised Hatfield's youthful, personal, and sincere actions. *Look* magazine, in its 7 March issue, listed Hatfield as a worthy "dark horse" candidate for the presidency. And noted novelist James Michener, thinking of becoming politically active, listed Hatfield among the

American political leaders he would be "proud at any time to be 'mixed up with.'" All of these salutes in the face of the harsh criticisms he sometimes received must have been satisfying to Hatfield, but he did not respond publicly to either the negative or positive comments. But Republican voters in Oregon did, giving Hatfield the ultimate salute, a 174,811 to 37,306 victory over his primary opponent, H. G. Atvater.

True, Hatfield was deeply involved in politics in the first half of 1962, but he was eyebrow deep in other happenings too. For instance, the governor was also busy trying to draw tourists to Oregon. Realizing that visitors to the Seattle World's Fair from April to October might be traveling over completed sections of I-5 or I-80, Hatfield called for a "hospitality conference" to encourage tourism. A few days later he made explicit that the "welcome mat" was out. In May, to make everything clear, Hatfield issued a chamber-of-commerce-like statement that Oregon newspapers carried: "This summer Oregon will become a tourist corridor to the Seattle World's Fair. We'll have an opportunity to impress an unusually great number of visitors with Oregon as a vacationland, as well as a wonderful place to work and live."

Speech making and visits to conferences continued unabated. One presentation captured headlines and led to Hatfield comments more than forty years later. When the graduating class at the elementary school at Shaw, a small village about ten miles southeast of Salem, invited the governor to speak at their graduation of six students, he agreed, even though after accepting he was invited to present at a much larger, more important group. He kept his promise to the Shaw students, urged them to be courageous, to work hard, and to keep their faith in God. He encouraged students to think of George Washington and Abraham Lincoln as models of character and action to follow. Later, Hatfield pointed to this unusual commitment and follow-through as the type of promise and action that he wanted to be remembered for and that it had helped him to expand his political recognition throughout the state.

In the second half of 1962, political momentum, as the weeks passed, escalated to the mountain top. Democratic candidate Thornton began throwing sharp darts at Hatfield. The governor, Thornton asserted, had been "preaching economy while he doubled the cost of running the government." Plus, Hatfield had more campaign funding because he catered to big businesses. Thornton then added that Hatfield had been out of state for 146 days in his first two years as governor, all the while "seeking the Republican nomination for vice president."

On most occasions Hatfield did not respond to Thornton's criticisms while laying out his campaign strategies. He told the Republican state central committee that he would "stress the importance of a strong economy" and would attempt to "build business confidence in government." He hoped, too, to change President Kennedy's disastrous handling of lumber and logging affairs in Oregon. In a few situations, Hatfield could be more critical of Thornton. He thought the attorney general's speeches contained "inaccuracies," and that Thornton had issued "lousy, phony opinions." Even more negative were the comments of Howell Appling, Oregon secretary of state and Hatfield's campaign manager. Appling told fellow Republicans, in referring to Thornton, "incompetence in one office [attorney general] is a poor recommendation for another."

Meanwhile, Hatfield was profiting from multiple positive comments from a variety of sources. The *Oregonian* backed Hatfield's projected tax plans, and A. Robert Smith, *Oregonian* correspondent in Washington, pronounced that Hatfield "looked good" at the governors' national conference. The short-lived new magazine *USA-1* was even more positive in an article on Hatfield titled "Favorite Son from Oregon" in its July issue. The author, Jonathan Rinehart, traced Hatfield's life from the moral shapings of his parents and his early political desires. "I always had a great ambition for a political career," he told the reporter, although his father wanted him to be a preacher and his mother, a doctor. The writer continued that Hatfield's "noticeable vigor" had won widespread support, and his moral uprightness had won hundreds of "Oregon's fundamentalists," southerners and normally Democrats, to the Republican Hatfield. Even though the governor's accomplishments were no more than "creditable but limited," he would remain a likely national candidate if he won decisively in the fall. *Time* magazine agreed that a decisive win over Thornton would enlarge Hatfield's national attention. In the 14 September issue in a piece titled "A Low-Key Campaigner," the writer spoke of Hatfield gaining national attention because he "avoided controversy, [and] concentrated instead on souping up the state's economy." And he had done what few Republicans had done: won support of labor organizations. The *Time* author predicted that Hatfield had done so very well that with a win in the fall he "might well be a top prospect for the No. 2 spot" on the Republican ticket in 1964.

Politics dominated the scene for Hatfield but did not capture all his time and abundant energies. Throughout 1962, the governor initiated several meetings to try to settle labor disputes. On these occasions he invited representatives from unions and management to his office to work out conflicts. Not all these attempts at mediation went well, but laborers and business leaders, largely, remained Hatfield supporters. He also had to deal with huge emotional issues surrounding a scheduled execution. Forty-one-year-old LeeRoy Sanford McGahuey had been sentenced to death for murdering a mother and child. After examining all the issues of the horrific case and even though he opposed capital punishment, Hatfield allowed the execution to take place. He had a "higher duty," he explained, in "carrying out . . . the people's will as expressed in the Constitution, statutes, and court proceedings." Established law trumped the governor's personal preference. Still, nearly forty years later he could not forget the incident, remembering the traumatic case as one of "Inheriting the Doomed."

Then, nature, in one of its most dramatic moments in Oregon history, blew politics off kilter. On 12 October, a violent storm hit with the fury of a vicious hurricane. It dealt unimaginable destruction and death along its twenty-four-hour, 1,500-mile dangerous path from northern California to British Columbia. Gusts of wind clocking over 100 miles an hour pummeled southern Oregon, Eugene, Salem, and Portland. Along the entire route, tens of thousands of trees (enough to frame more than one million homes) were knocked down, 53,000 homes damaged or destroyed, and sixty-three lives lost. In Oregon alone, twenty-four were dead, millions of dollars of damage wrought, 3 billion board feet of lumber damaged, and 496,000 families left without power. It was, obviously, the worst wind storm to hit the West Coast.

Governor Hatfield moved quickly to deal with the natural disaster. Politics was put on hold, the national guard ordered into action, and emergency funding made available. During the hectic days immediately following the Columbus Day storm, Hatfield refused to campaign for reelection, instead focusing his energies on needed help for the beleaguered state and its citizens. Most Oregonians saluted the governor's actions, with a few suggesting he could have done more and more expeditiously.

With less than a month remaining before the looming elections, the state politicians were soon back at work, most often, unfortunately, downgrading opponents rather than touting their own strengths and achievements. Democrat Thornton fired familiar shots at Republican Hatfield. The attorney general charged that the governor's hiring of a legal aide, Loren Hicks, at the state's expense was an unconstitutional act. He also pointed to Hatfield's numerous out-of-state junkets as wrong and, Thornton added, done largely to boost Hatfield's chances for a national office. Moreover, the governor spoke falsely about the Oregonian economy; the state's "rate of business failure," Thornton asserted, was "the highest rate" in the country. In addition, by cutting taxes by 20 percent on timber companies, the governor had unfairly added to the tax burdens of other residents in the timber counties.

For the most part, Hatfield chose not to respond to Thornton's charged accusations. He did urge the attorney general to take the case of Loren Hicks to court if he wished. Thornton did not, stating that the governor's statements were merely a "stunt" to gain attention. As election time drew nearer, Thornton also castigated the state's newspapers for not giving him as much headline attention as Hatfield received.

Throughout the fall, most political prognosticators predicted that Hatfield would win reelection comfortably in November. They were right: on 6 November, Hatfield received 345,497, or 54.2 percent of the votes; Thornton got 265,359, or 41.63 percent. Independent candidate Robert H. Wampler gained 26,142, or 4.1 percent. Keeping in mind that registered Oregon Democrats outnumbered the state's Republicans by 75,000–80,000, that meant Hatfield won over not only nearly all of his fellow Republicans but also a surprising number of Democratic voters. If not a landside, Hatfield's win was an "easy victory," as one journalist put it.

Mark Hatfield had kept his promise: he would run for reelection to the governor's chair, not for another and perhaps higher position. Having won, he was, to that point, Oregon's only two-term governor since 1900.

4

Oregon Governor, Second Term, 1963–1967

On the cold, wintery Monday of 14 January 1963, reelected Governor Hatfield stood before the Oregon state legislature to deliver his second inaugural address. He hoped to warm up support for several of his key plans among members of the predominantly Democratic state senate and house. Some of these proposals were not new; legislators had heard and considered them in 1959 and 1961. Some even dated back to Hatfield's own time in the legislature. The content of the address belies depictions of Hatfield as a runaway liberal Republican, always pushing for new and novel ideas. Rather, mostly the opposite. As the address revealed again, once Hatfield backed an idea he rarely let it go, seemingly convinced that given another opportunity a recently defeated idea could still win its way through the legislature.

Even before Hatfield appeared before the Oregon lawmakers, he had detailed much of what he would offer there. In the two months between his reelection in early November and the opening of the Fifty-Second Oregon Legislative Assembly, Hatfield had disclosed most of his intended budget and political agenda. The governor's burgeoning budget engendered immediate debate.

The biennial budget for 1963–65 was pegged at an eye-popping $405 million, up nearly $40 million from the two-year budget of 1961. When opponents quickly slammed the huge—they said bloated—request, Hatfield defended himself by explaining that his budget was $90 million less than the state agencies had requested. Finances in Oregon were increasingly tight. Previous surpluses ranging back to post–World War II days had vanished, and education and welfare costs, especially, were skyrocketing. Additional funding was necessary to fulfill state economic needs. Quarrels over budget matters would disrupt Oregon politics through winter and spring of 1963—and until the end of the year.

Educational demands were at the center of arising emotional conflicts. Hatfield was asking for a great deal. The educational segment of the budget would run to nearly $241 million, about 59 percent of the entire amount. That expanding request was $39 million above the 1961 budget. In his requests for education, Hatfield included a thousand new positions in higher education because college enrollments had boomed, doubling in the past eight years. He also lobbied for better salaries at all levels for teachers. Beyond the budget, the governor called for an additional $45 million in bonds to fund new buildings, which he hoped Oregon voters would support in a special election.

These escalating figures upset several legislative leaders. Opponents of the educational requests spoke harshly against that large part of the governor's budget. Democratic state senator Richard Eymann labeled Hatfield's budget "phony" because the call for bonds for educational buildings was not in the budget and because the governor had also built in $7 million in deficit spending in his request. That should not be, Eymann asserted. Other Democratic leaders, while not using Eymann's words also had reservations about the proposed spending for education.

Others reacted more positively to Hatfield's recommended budget. The *Oregonian,* a Republican newspaper most often supporting the governor, described his budget as "minimal and tight." Since an "education avalanche has struck," the newspaper noted, the legislature must find the monies to support educational needs, else "a major breakdown in education" would occur. Political journalist Merwin Shoemaker agreed. He predicted that the new legislature would face "the roughest financial winter of the state's history" and called on legislators in Salem to step up to face these pressing needs.

Hatfield's projected tax policies also stirred up differences. Most of his tax measures were repeats of previous ideas. The governor spoke often for his so-called net receipts form of taxation, which would "widen the tax base" by taxing incomes and sales of most Oregonians, thereby raising more revenue and lessening tax pressures on the middle class. If Hatfield's net receipts plan were implemented, it would raise about $23 million. Democratic house speaker Clarence Barton supported the tax measure, whereas Democratic president of the senate Ben Musa, an accountant, opposed Hatfield, calling the plan disguised "gross receipts" taxation.

Less controversial was Hatfield's request to levy a new 4 cent tax on each package of cigarettes, which would raise approximately $13 million. This was a new tax in Oregon, the only state without a cigarette tax. At first, nearly everyone in the legislature supported this proposed tax.

Combined, these two tax measures would have brought in $36 million. Together, these revenues would have taken care of most of the additional funding Hatfield estimated that Oregon needed in its 1963–65 budget.

Other parts of Hatfield's agenda placed before the legislature also contained a familiar ring. Chief among these was his call for cabinet-like reorganization of the state's executive branch. The call for reorganization had not gone well in the 1961 legislature. Rock-solid Democrats castigated the move as an attempted power grab by the governor. Hatfield countered that his reorganization plan would streamline the executive branch, make it less expensive, and allow the governor to move more decisively as the state's chief executive. He also called for the new cabinet-like leaders to be governor appointees. In addition, the secretary of state and state treasurer would no longer be elected by Oregon voters but named by the governor.

Perhaps Hatfield realized, as he noted later, that he had "tried to do too much too quickly," so he revised his reorganization plan presented in January 1963. Now he called for but two cabinet-like organizations, the Department of Natural Resources and the Department of Commerce. Without saying so, Hatfield had returned to another one of his often-tried techniques: if he could not get his whole agenda in the first try, he would attempt to get it piece by piece in a series of tries.

Finally, a previously organized committee would present a rewritten constitution for the legislature's consideration. Hatfield was convinced the state's present constitution was out of date, cumbersome, and in several ways a hodge-podge of amendments thrown together over time. It needed updating.

Party divisions in the new legislature of 1963 were similar to those of 1959 and 1961. Democrats controlled the body. In the senate, Democrats held twenty-one seats, Republicans nine; in the house, Democrats maintained a slight lead of thirty-one to twenty-nine over the Republicans. But the Democrats were clearly divided into more liberal and conservative wings. Over time, Hatfield realized—and followed up on his realization—that he could, and did, appeal more to conservative than to liberal Democrats. In gaining the attention of Democratic conservatives, he could achieve more of a numerical balance between the two parties.

At the legislature's opening, then, Hatfield especially pushed the previously mentioned measures. He urged both chambers to adopt a net receipts plan of taxation that would broaden the tax base to include nearly all Oregonians. He supported the burgeoning requests of educational leaders, especially those in higher education, to enlarge their budgets to address expanding enrollments and raise low teacher and professor salaries. He also backed plans to revise the Oregon constitution and to establish a cabinet-like system of executive departments whose leaders would be appointed by the governor .

Several segments of Hatfield's budget plans and agenda were soon under legislative consideration and almost immediately stirred up escalating conflicts. In fact, in the longest Oregon legislature on record to that time—stretching from 14 January to 3 June, 141 days—the session was a journey of continuing disappointment for Hatfield. Almost none of his agenda made it through the legislature, at least not in the form he had presented to the Salem lawmakers. Gradually emerging in these long weeks was a major power war between Hatfield and the Joint Ways and Means Committee, under the no-give-way Democratic leadership of cochairmen senator Ward Cook of Portland and representative Ross Morgan of Gresham. These two legislators and their numerous supporters were not about to allow a strong executive like Hatfield to dominate the legislative branch. The house and senate members of the committee took on the governor's ideas, opposed many of them, and revised several others. Seen whole, the fifty-second legislature was a stretch of downtime for Hatfield. Nearly all of his agenda and budget was dismissed or dramatically altered.

Taxation policies—how to raise the state's needed revenues—took up more legislative time and energy than any other issue. Hatfield estimated that his net receipts plan and the 4-cent cigarette tax would together add up to $36 million of the $40 million needed to cover his proposed budget in the coming biennium. It was not to be. The senate, dominated by Democrats, and the house, where Republicans were much stronger, hammered out separate tax plans as the weeks wore on. Neither of the plans had much resemblance to Hatfield's tax ideas. Frustrated because the legislature seemed unable to settle on a tax plan, Hatfield criticized the group as a "do nothing" legislature, echoing what an upset President Harry Truman had labeled the U.S. Congress more than a decade earlier. Hatfield's blunt criticisms even alienated some of his fellow Republicans trying to sponsor his policies.

Controversies surrounding educational matters were equally uncomfortable for the governor. Although Hatfield had reduced the budgetary requests of higher education and public school groups, generally he strongly supported educational measures. He had, for example, reduced the request of the Higher Education Board from $96 million to $82 million, but the Ways and Means Committee threatened to cut the total another $13 million. The committee raised the student-faculty ratio on college campuses from 16:1 to 17:1 and lowered any salary raises for faculty to achieve the cut of $13 million. Nor was the legislature willing to send Oregon voters a large bond initiative to build new campus buildings. Hatfield, upset with these large reductions, angrily accused the legislature of taking the "meat cleaver" to his budget. As political journalist Merwin Shoemaker put it, the contest over educational funding was "easily the big financial battle of 1963."

Hatfield hoped the legislature would accept his call for a rewritten Oregon constitution. A revision committee had labored for more than a year trying to revise the original 1857 constitution, cutting out overlapping and vague phrasing as well as out-of-date stipulations. The committee had also followed Hatfield's encouragement in placing more appointive power in the hands of the governor and moving toward a cabinet-like organization for the executive branch. Unfortunately for Hatfield the recommended revised constitution met a similar fate as Hatfield's plans on taxation and education.

Once the revised document was introduced, controversy stormed on the scene. Varied negative reactions to separate parts of the proposed constitution reverberated through the legislature. Democrats reacted in opposition to the new powers the document would give to the governor, including his authority to appoint leaders of executive branches. Others thought the reorganization of the state's voting districts was no improvement on the existing version of the constitution. As part of the revision, Hatfield's push for a Department of Natural Resources alienated sportsmen and gradually lost support, although the governor was able to salvage a new Department of Commerce, one of the few victories Hatfield enjoyed in early 1963.

Even though Hatfield had not said much about the state's civil defense program, a legislative decision on that group stirred up as much controversy as any other judgment. The Ways and Means Committee slashed the proposed defense budget from $410,000 to $50,000 and in doing so raised the ire of the governor. Opponents of the civil defense program pointed to its obvious failures during the Columbus Day storm that ravaged the state with deadly and destructive winds as the reason for dramatically cutting its budget. The drastic curtailing of civil defense funding would force staff reduction from eighteen to three persons. Discouraged and upset, Hatfield nonetheless urged civil defense supporters to "pick up the pieces of the shambles which the legislature has left." The governor and other like-minded political leaders hoped the federal government might step in to fill some of the large gap in funding for civil defense the Oregon legislature had created. That proved a vain hope.

Newspapers on 29 May revealed a low point for Hatfield in his contentious competitions with the state legislature. On that day he had to face the essential destruction of the civil defense program as it had been known, and at the same time he was informed that the senate had killed his proposal for a new constitution. Adding to the misery, the tax bill passed had little to do with the tax proposals Hatfield had proposed in January.

Even though Hatfield did not so state publicly, he must have been greatly disappointed and frustrated with the legislature. So little of his agenda had been followed; the budget that was passed, although similar in amount to his proposal, was greatly revised in specifics. Yet, seen in later perspective, the outcome is not surprising. The opposing Democrats were in control numerically, holding fifty-two of the legislature's ninety seats. The remaining thirty-eight Republicans would have difficulty passing any legislation with their smaller numbers. Plus, many of the Democrats were set in not letting the newly reelected Republican governor Hatfield augment his already growing power. Hatfield's defeats here stemmed as much from clear partisanship as from inferior numbers. Taken together, those two forces dominated the Oregon political scene in early 1963.

In the hurly-burly of the legislative months, Hatfield had little time aside from his almost daily contacts with Salem politicians. He still managed, however, to keep his hectic schedule of travel and speech making. He flew east to work out agreements with Senator Morse, gave Lincoln Day speeches in California, and presented a much-publicized speech at the Western Governors' Convention in Arizona in April. The latter talk stirred up the most controversy, especially among conservative Republicans, when Hatfield spoke of far-right conservatives as being like fascists. These right-wingers "are here now," Hatfield told the governors, and they were "a danger to American ideals." Later, commentators emphasized that Hatfield had made this speech roundly criticizing hard-right conservatives in Barry Goldwater's backyard.

Hatfield's comfortable reelection margin, his added TV appearances, and his continuing speech making expanded his national reputation. Gallup polls during the winter and spring months listed him as a Republican presidential possibility for 1964, usually ranked after Rockefeller, Goldwater, and governors George Romney of Michigan and William W.

Scranton of Pennsylvania. The *U.S. News and World Report* also named Hatfield as one of the possible candidates for 1964. Even the noted writer Gore Vidal gave Hatfield a presidential plug in the March *Esquire*. At first when asked about his favored Republican candidate for the next election, Hatfield supported Rockefeller, but soon thereafter Rocky's controversial divorce and quick remarriage undercut the New York governor's popularity across the country. When Oregon Republicans exhibited a growing fondness for Goldwater, Hatfield seemed satisfied to accept Goldwater as a possible candidate. When interviewers pushed Hatfield for his opinions about becoming a presidential or vice-presidential candidate, the governor waffled, telling the journalists that he had no plan for a candidacy, but if support for either of the offices came his way he would certainly listen and consider such a possibility. Even though Hatfield's critics fired shots at him for trying to grab national office, the governor did not speak widely about or participate in national affairs.

Instead, Hatfield found time to support some of his favorite entities and to push Oregon. He looked after the lumber industry, trying to get the Kennedy administration to protect Oregon loggers from escalating Canadian competition and to lower taxes on logging areas in the state. He encouraged labor members, too, to work first with the governor's office should they feel mistreated and want to go on strike. Several of his speeches of the time were "sales jobs" encouraging business expansion in Oregon. As an example, he spoke of the huge new Hilton Hotel in downtown Portland as just the kind of entrepreneurial action the state needed. Nor did Hatfield let up on his support for a graduate center in Portland. He noted how much a firm like Tektronix could benefit from such a center.

From early June to the end of year, controversial hangovers from the legislative session in Salem buried Hatfield in long, involved political contests. The most emotional and time-consuming were those concerning taxation measures and the biennial budget. Upset that the legislature had not adopted any of his tax plans and had put together a jumbled, almost haphazard tax measure to raise the total of the needed $405 million dollars, Hatfield chose a halfway response: he would not veto the legislature's method of revenue raising, but neither would he support it. He passed on the lawmakers' plan by not signing it and thus allowing it to become law.

Events in the summer concerning the tax controversy would eventually force Hatfield to move in still another direction. Outspoken journalist J. Francyl Howard, publisher of Albany and Corvallis newspapers and dead-set opponent of the legislature's tax measures, decided to refer the measures to the public. Moving quickly and energetically, Howard secured 55,000 signatures, almost twice the number needed for a referendum to voters. And the voters made their views abundantly clear, voting by a seven to two margin on 15 October to reject the legislature's tax bill.

These events pushed Hatfield into several turnabouts. Rather than adhere to his earlier, let-alone position on the legislature's tax measures, Hatfield now opposed the proposed referendum, evidently thinking that action might lead to something even worse. But once the referendum was secured and showed Oregonians' strong support for something different, Hatfield switched again. The referendum vote, the governor stated, was "a mandate from the people."

Now several options faced Hatfield. He could call a special session of the legislature but wondered if that would not lead to more wrangling and upset. Or, he could ask the legislature to allow him to make the necessary budget cuts so that the legislature-passed taxes would be unnecessary. When critics dismissed allowing the governor to make the necessary cuts, Hatfield called for a special session to convene on 11 November.

The special session, lasting from 11 November to 2 December, led to several surprising results. The dramatic assassination of President John F. Kennedy on 22 November and the following national mourning, Hatfield's absence to attend Kennedy's funeral, and the Thanksgiving holiday led to a longer session than planned. The central decision came down to whether the legislature would make the necessary cuts to reduce their earlier budget or allow the governor to make the cuts. Unexpectedly, the legislature allowed Hatfield to do the trimming but limited the changes to two areas: he would reduce the budget from $404 million to $361 million by major cuts in agency and school budgets and include a stop-gap measure to change the ways employers remitted their withholding taxes. Most unusual was the absence of criticism, partisanship, and division that had characterized the fifty-second legislature earlier in the year. Some thought that both the legislature and governor, sensing the will of Oregon voters, decided to compromise, work together, and get the job done.

A few other issues captured Hatfield's attention in the midst of the tax and budget controversies. He became more involved in national politics, and here another change took place. During his earlier years as Oregon governor, Hatfield was increasingly identified—and himself identified—with New York governor Nelson Rockefeller. Oregon writers often spoke of the two governors as leading lights on the left side of the Republican spectrum. Hatfield had met with Rockefeller and had supported him as a Republican of the highest order, in every way worthy of the party's presidential candidate. Then Rockefeller's controversial divorce and remarriage came about. On 4 May 1963, he married Margaretta "Happy" Murphy. One month earlier Rockefeller had led his major rival, Arizona senator Barry Goldwater, by a 43 to 23 percent margin. One week after the marriage, Rockefeller's lead had dwindled to six points, and by July Goldwater led in the Republican race 31 to 27 percent.

Oregonians endorsed the fall of Rockefeller and the rise of Goldwater. By midsummer, Oregon journalists were predicting the political death of Rockefeller and the crowning of Goldwater. This rapid shift put Governor Hatfield in a tough spot. Always something of a pragmatist, despite his parallel commitment to conscience and promises, Hatfield could see the writing on the wall. He stopped taking sides; now he would wait until the 1964 elections and support the candidate the GOP chose. By the end of 1963, Hatfield was firmly in the uncommitted, middle-of-the-road position, speaking for both Rockefeller and Goldwater as strong, supportable candidates.

These trends in national politics often included Hatfield, although usually tangentially and more often in Oregon than outside the state. The governor nearly always begged off on a specific comment when asked about his chances as a presidential or, more often, a vice-presidential nominee. Even though journalists inside and beyond Oregon spoke of Hatfield as a "dark horse" candidate, he refused to encourage his home state to launch him as a "favorite son" candidate in 1964. Yet in late August, the San Francisco *Examiner* declared that Hatfield was "gaining stature" in the GOP, and three weeks later political journalist A. Robert Smith revealed that, although Hatfield would not be a "favorite son" out of Oregon, he did plan to run for the U.S. Senate in 1966. That was the sole reference in the media to such a possibility for Hatfield.

Political leaders also came to Oregon, and Hatfield attended a national governors' conference, both of which provided further contact with national figures. While still in the White House, President Kennedy had visited the Tongue Point area to the east of Astoria and flew over the projected Dunes park area on the Oregon coast. Nelson Rockefeller and Barry Goldwater came to a political conference in Eugene, and Hatfield attended a governors' conference in Miami where he and Rockefeller pushed hard for a

Hatfield and workers. Hatfield's strong connection with laborers and labor unions was unusual for an Oregon Republican in the 1950s and 1960s. Workers supported Hatfield in several elections. Photo provided by Lincoln County Historical Society and OSU Libraries Special Collections and Archives Research Center, A 98.33.511cN2678.

civil rights program that the more numerous Democratic governors, chiefly those from the South, blocked.

Even a few nonpolitical subjects gained Hatfield's attention. He continued to support the possible graduate research center in Portland as it wobbled uncertainly for lack of specific funding. At a couple of cultural celebrations, Hatfield and Native American groups in Oregon displayed their mutual regard for one another. Noted TV interviewer Charles Collingwood came to Salem to converse with Hatfield, a conversation that drew a good deal of newspaper comment.

And in the months from June to the end of the year, Hatfield's participation in several events displayed once again his tendency toward middle-of-the-road positions. He urged labor groups to meet with their employers for negotiation rather than strike quickly. He encouraged game fishermen not to push for shutting down commercial fishing and putting people out of work. And for loggers and farmers, he also sought to find compromises in their challenges to meeting changing economic conditions. Throughout these months Hatfield continued to push Oregonians economically, not to become "extinct" in lethargy and laziness. In the closing months of the year, newspapers celebrated the Hatfield family with numerous photos of the governor, his vivacious wife, and their two adorable children. The governor sent out a year-ending Christmas message urging Oregonians to remember and follow the teachings of Jesus Christ, so central to the governor's own life.

In early January 1964, news broadcasters Walter Cronkite, Chet Huntley, and others joined Mark Hatfield for a buffet in New York City. The lively conversation included talk of whether Hatfield would be named chairman of the upcoming Republican national convention the next summer or be one of the two nominees on the GOP national ticket. The New York meeting was but prologue for the escalating notoriety of Hatfield as an increasingly recognized national political figure in the first half of 1964.

As year number two of Hatfield's second gubernatorial term unfolded, two events gradually captured most of his time and energy. The first and more surprising event was Hatfield's important and central role in the upcoming national Republican convention in midsummer 1964. The second, and less unusual event, the presidential election the following November, did much to clarify what would be Hatfield's position in the Republican Party. Taken together, these two events enlarged Hatfield's political reputation well beyond the state of Oregon. But, of course, they did not tell the full story of another action-filled year in the governor's leadership.

Even in the opening weeks of 1964, Oregon journalists were speculating about what Hatfield's role would be in the Republication nominating convention in July. Would he, near the top of the heap, be chosen as the convention chairman, or, more likely, the temporary chairman, to open the convention? Was there a possibility that he would even be selected to deliver the keynote address, a limelight position often saved for a young newcomer who could capture the attention of party loyalists but also that of independent voters thus far undecided about their presidential candidate? Mark Hatfield fit the description of the keynoter, but neither the party nor the governor said anything about that possibility in the first months of 1964.

The breaking news came in May. Hatfield would fill two roles: he would open the convention as the temporary chairman, but, more important, he would deliver the keynote address. The Republican higher-ups had decided that Hatfield, the handsome, charismatic westerner, should give the speech and serve as the temporary chairman. But Thruston Morton, an eastern Republican warhorse, would be the regular convention chairman.

In the two months stretching from Hatfield's being named until he delivered the keynote address on 13 July in the famed Cow Palace in San Francisco, the governor was busy deciding the content of the notable speech. He looked at the writings of his boyhood hero Herbert Hoover, read several works on American history, checked the ideas of Abraham Lincoln, and even spoke to former president Dwight Eisenhower about what he should say. Information from these sources found their way into the speech.

The rousing presentation, "Faith Not Fear," exhibited Hatfield's rhetorical power that Oregonians had known for nearly fifteen years. In the first half of the speech the governor, as expected, sliced up the Democrats for their negative, debilitating "fears." Then, in the second half, he praised the several "faiths" that motivated and drove his fellow Republicans.

In his sharp criticism of Democrats, Hatfield pointed to three fears the party displayed: "fear of facts," "fear of the future," and "fear of the people." The Democratic cover-ups of party leaders in high places and false and unfulfilled promises illustrated fear of facts. In their deadening ties to the past and their lack of progressive spirit, Democratic leaders exemplified their fear of the future. In their unwillingness to name the war that was unraveling Vietnam and increasingly involving the United States and refusing to allow individuals to make their own decisions, the party of Lyndon Johnson was demonstrating its fear of the people.

Not surprisingly, when Hatfield turned to his fellow Republicans, the party of faith, he found much to praise. Republicans were, the governor stated, the party of the people, interested in the "cause of freedom" and the "principles of morality." His political group (and here Hatfield was echoing Republican presidential candidate's Barry Goldwater's words) offered a choice between fear and faith. The Republicans, the party of Abraham Lincoln, Theodore Roosevelt, Herbert Hoover, and Dwight Eisenhower, welcomed migrants and immigrants, supported free enterprise, strong global leadership, and a nourishing religious heritage—in short, a "pilgrimage of faith."

The most remembered—and controversial—portion of the address came in Hatfield's comments condemning right-wing organizations. Americans cherished the rights inherited from the Declaration of Independence, which included political, civil, and religious rights. But forces were trying to destroy our freedoms, wrapping themselves "in a false cloak of patriotism or an equally false cloak of religion." And then the words that brought cheers from supporters and boos from opponents: "There are bigots in this nation who spew forth the venom of hate. They parade under hundreds of labels, including the Communist party, including the Ku Klux Klan and the John Birch Society." All these groups must be opposed and defeated; instead, follow the path of faith, which the Republicans offered, sponsored, and defended.

Strong responses to Hatfield's keynote address were not long in coming. In fact, nearly six weeks later Hatfield was still receiving up to one hundred letters a day, mostly positive but some very negative. Not a few Republican conservatives, mostly strong supporters of Barry Goldwater, criticized the governor for his condemning remarks about the John Birch Society. Some letter writers, both conservative Republicans and members of the John Birch Society, were especially harsh in their reactions to Hatfield's speech.

Others were much more positive. The *Oregonian* offered clear praise for the keynoter. Although Hatfield "will not become a Goldwater type," wrote political columnist Herbert Lundy, he "will work for Republican victory in November." Even though both the conservative and liberal wings were taking "shots at Mark" because of the content of his opening address, he would steer the course between the two extremes and campaign for his party—and for Goldwater. Associated Press writer Bob Thomas agreed, stating, "Hatfield, reportedly chosen to present a youthful image for the Republicans, fulfilled that function well." Television broadcasters Chet Huntley and David Brinkley also thought Hatfield had done well in San Francisco. Reporters for the *Los Angeles Times* and *Hollywood Reporter* had similar thoughts. As expected of a keynoter, he labeled the Democrats as a set of backward-looking rascals covering up their shortcomings, and then he moved on to salute the strengths of his Republicans. Back in Oregon, Ethel O'Dell, an eastern Oregon resident, undoubtedly spoke like many of that state's voters when she said that even though she was "not a dedicated Republican and would never vote for

Goldwater," she supported Hatfield. His keynote presentation reminded her of how much she liked her governor. She was "proud of his thinking, proud of his delivery of his thoughts, proud of his looks, proud that he belongs to Oregon. Proud of Mark Hatfield."

Hatfield kept his promises, rallying Republicans and supporting Goldwater in the next three to four months. Unlike fellow progressive Republicans such as Rockefeller, George Romney, and William Scranton, Hatfield did not pull away from Goldwater. He saluted the Arizona senator as superior to President Johnson as a leader, honest politician, and moral man. Some wondered if Hatfield kept to his middle-of-the-road trail—pushing the Republicans *and* Barry Goldwater—for his own purposes. Already having decided to run for the Senate in 1966, Hatfield, these observers noted, was presenting himself as a loyal Republican but also a man who could unite liberals and conservatives.

In fall 1964, Hatfield bounced around Oregon like an indefatigable salesman giving speeches. The challenge was doubly daunting; the governor had to keep abreast of his executive duties, and polls were predicting that Goldwater was running well behind President Johnson, with a landslide victory for the Democrat in the White House in the offing. The message of Hatfield's political agenda remained the same: though he had some differences in outlook from Goldwater, he supported his party's candidate. Plus, Goldwater stood with Hatfield in keeping the deciding power at the state level; both criticized the burgeoning and overreaching central government that the Democrats supported and nurtured. Hatfield even loaned his virtuoso publicity man, Travis Cross, to the Goldwater campaign to further the Republican reach.

The predictions of pollsters that Johnson would "snow" Goldwater proved to be on target. Johnson captured just over 43 million votes (61 percent) to Goldwater's 27 million plus (39 percent). Johnson's electoral margin—486 to

Hatfield as campaigner. Early in his political career, Hatfield vowed to become a nonstop campaigner. He would speak often, visit towns and schools, and make sure to shake hands with as many voters as possible. OSU Libraries Special Collections and Archives Research Center, P0 61 SG1 73.

52—was even more eye-popping. The popular vote in Oregon gave Johnson a wider margin: 501,000 (64 percent) to 283,000 (36 percent). Overall, Johnson's national win was the most one-sided since Franklin Roosevelt's landslide victory in 1936.

Hatfield did not say much about Goldwater and the huge loss in November 1964. Rather, in postelection days he talked a good deal about a needed restructuring of the Republican Party, placing more emphases on moderate to progressive stances. Without much mention of Goldwater's huge election loss, Hatfield pointed to the ideas of Rockefeller, Romney, and Scranton as models for the reorganization of the Republicans and a move to a more central or slightly left position.

Even though politics consumed most of Hatfield's time and energy in 1964, other ideas and events also gained his attention. For instance, he made use of his many speeches in Oregon to trumpet some of the stances at the center of the Republican Party. None was emphasized more than the need to keep ultimate power at the local level, where states and communities would be open to hearing and following citizens' desires. Such emphases would keep Americans out from under the huge, dominating lion's paw that Roosevelt and the New Deal stretched out in the 1930s and that Lyndon Johnson was replicating in the mid-1960s. Hatfield also was convinced the Republican Party was the most valued conduit through which American enterprise, augmented civil rights, and more realistic foreign affairs could be carried out.

Gradually, Hatfield was becoming more aware of conservation of natural resources. This growing awareness never led him as far as what was later labeled an "environmentalist," but instead to mediating positions. He supported loggers but kept in mind the needs and wants of logging companies; he listened to sports fishermen but maintained that those who fished for a living also merited his support. And he spoke of agreements among the governors of Washington, Idaho, and Oregon as a way to keep California from appropriating Northwest waters. In these positions, Hatfield represented one side of conservation thinking in play for more than half a century. President Theodore Roosevelt,

thoroughly influenced by his forester friend Gifford Pin-
chot, stood for "wise use" of natural resources. Assertive
conservationist John Muir spoke passionately for "wilderness" advocates: the setting aside of forests, lands, deserts,
and natural wonders as wilderness areas to be appreciated
but not "used." Hatfield was drawn to the wise-use philosophy, a position later enthusiastic environmentalists greatly
disliked.

One of Hatfield's most intriguing involvements with conservation matters concerned what Oregon coast promot-
ers called the "Twenty Miracle Miles" stretching along the
state's central coast roughly from the Salmon River mouth
to Depoe Bay. When Hatfield visited the area and viewed
the jumbles of weeds, garbage, and other throw-aways, he
relabeled the area "Twenty Miserable Miles." Although the
governor's rewording upset local enthusiasts, they and others in many areas of the state heard Hatfield and decided
to take on the "jumble" that desecrated so many areas of
Oregon.

Several times each month Hatfield appeared at the opening of a new business that had come to Oregon or of other
firms expanding or refurbishing their sites. He saw these as
opportunities to preach the gospel of Oregon as a premier
site for business and industry. When the famed 3M company built a site near Medford and a Job Corps site was
established at Tongue Point near Astoria, Hatfield was on
the scene to cheer for what had occurred and what, with the
expanding backing of Oregon leaders and voters, could happen. Immediately after the November presidential election,
Hatfield, his wife Antoinette, and staff members traveled to
Japan and Taiwan for two weeks of trade negotiations to
further business dealings between Asians and the state of
Oregon. In these events, Hatfield had become increasingly
a "public" governor.

These expanding leadership roles became clearer in
several other events. When Alaska suffered a devastating

9.2 earthquake in March, Hatfield engineered several actions to send support north. Even more important to Oregonians, when the worst floods the state had ever experienced shut down many highways, damaged homes and businesses, and virtually closed the state in the last two weeks of December and first week of January, Hatfield stood tall in directing government responses and aid to address the damage the huge walls of water rolling over the state had caused. The news pictured the governor, on Christmas day, staying in his office manning civil defense, national guard, and other groups to address threats throughout the coastal and Willamette Valley areas.

But alongside these leadership successes were several failures or examples of unfinished business. For instance, Hatfield seemed unable or unwilling to settle on a national park area on the Oregon coast, even though several plans had been introduced to him. He also favored a graduate center for research in Portland but seemed hesitant to push the effort.

These public events did not entirely dominate the governor's private life. Family continued very important to Hatfield. In early September, the governor and his wife welcomed their third child, daughter Theresa. News about Antoinette often appeared in state's newspapers. She was repeatedly depicted as an exceptionally attractive and lively young woman. Her hosting, her recipe making, and especially her dozens of unusual hats sometimes attracted as much public attention as the youthful governor. But for the most part Antoinette chose to remain off the scene politically, refusing to comment on political issues journalists put to her.

As usual, Mark Hatfield had in mind what he wanted to introduce to the legislature in early 1965 well before the lawmakers met in Salem in mid-January. He began to announce segments of his budget and legislative agenda soon after the presidential election in November and continued to unroll these plans up to the opening of the legislature on 11 January. He submitted a balanced $456 million budget, $97 million more than budgeted for 1963–65. Hatfield's agenda for the Fifty-Third Oregon Legislative Assembly was titled "The Greater Progress." Although his presentation cited—and praised—recent achievements in the state, the governor stressed most that legislators must think primarily of present needs and plans for the future. "Progress" in the past should lead to "progress" in the next few years.

Hatfield's opening speech before the legislature in January included several familiar policies and a few newer ones. The most familiar of Hatfield's proposals illustrated the governor's conviction that "an idea implanted in one session or one decade may not take root for years." His previously proposed measures included government reorganization, taxation policy, commercial and industrial development, and educational support. Also, as he had three times before, Hatfield urged legislators to complete a revision of Oregon's outdated and ill-organized state constitution. State agencies also needed restructuring to ensure greater efficiency and lower costs. Hatfield did not think new taxes were needed, but he did encourage lawmakers to adopt his net receipts tax policy to widen the state's tax base. Saluting economic achievements of the previous six years, Hatfield pushed for added attention—and support—for commercial and industrial development. Educational programs merited further attention and funding because school and college populations were expanding. Hatfield again spoke for the graduate research center and supported greater financial support for the state's burgeoning community colleges.

Hatfield's "Greater Progress" presentation on 11 January also added new segments to his agenda. He stressed highway needs more than previously, especially substandard secondary highways. The governor, in addition, pointed to several facets of the state's and region's water policies that necessitated further study. Dissatisfied with mounting juvenile and prison problems, Hatfield asked for a corrections division to address these troubling areas. He was more insistent, too, about examining problems concerning political reapportionment, equal rights, and the medical needs of seniors. Noting the appearance of President Lyndon Johnson's new War on Poverty policies, Hatfield pointed legislators to places and programs where Oregon might work closely with the federal government in these areas of concern. Finally, Hatfield was convinced that county governments merited additional support but, he added, there ought to be fewer local governments so as to ensure greater efficiency and encourage cost cutting.

The new legislature opened on 11 January and ended its work on 14 May, only to be called into special session for a few days the following week. In its first few weeks, the new body seemed to be quite different from the fractious, controversial Fifty-Second. The new legislators brought a new spirit of compromise and less partisan contention. In the four legislatures Hatfield worked with, this was the only one in which his Republicans controlled one branch of the legislature. This time it was the house, where Hatfield's party occupied thirty-two seats to the Democrats' twenty-eight. In addition, Hatfield had a more friendly senate than previously. A coalition of eleven Republicans and six conservative Democrats, led by senate president Harry D. Boivin (D, Klamath Falls), outnumbered the thirteen remaining Democrats, allowing Hatfield often to gain the support of the senate. Another difference proved valuable: the opinionated Ways and Means Committee was less obstreperous in 1965 than in 1963. Some observers thought the negative reactions of Oregon voters to the actions and ideas of the fifty-second legislature encouraged this key committee to be less combative and more willing to compromise with Hatfield.

Hatfield was happy with the legislature's activity in the first months of 1965, praising their quick, good actions and harmonious working. By the end of March the governor, while still praising the actions of the house under Monte Montgomery's leadership, was beginning to have reservations about the senate. The mistaken attitude of the solons, Hatfield thought, was "the less action, the less boat rocking, the better the record of achievement." The senators were too satisfied with "the status quo." Still, the lawmakers were moving forward and likely would achieve more than the previous Salem gathering because "they are not playing political poker."

Hatfield's agenda issues that captured more positive attention than any other were those dealing with water policies. Legislators in both houses seemed to agree with Hatfield on water issues. The governor called for a comprehensive study of Oregon's water resources—in light of the escalating water needs of California and other southwestern areas. In urging funding for water planning, Hatfield seemed to agree with one senator's comments that some thought "history is written in blood, but the history of Oregon is being written in water." Later, in a meeting of western governors, Hatfield told the state executives that they must view water needs from a regional perspective and well into the future. On this subject the governor and the legislators were in step, with the Salem lawmakers providing the requested funds for research and planning dealing with water policies.

On the question of mandated congressional redistricting, Hatfield and the lawmakers were at the opposite end of negotiation; they could not find an acceptable compromise in nearly 124 days of sessions. The governor pushed the legislators to follow the Supreme Court's guidelines of one-man, one-vote, meaning trying to equalize as close as possible the number of voters in each of Oregon's four congressional districts. The key issue, which no one including the governor wanted to admit, was that the lawmakers wanted the redistricting, if carried out, to favor and support their home areas. Finally, in the governor's specially called session, a compromise suggested by house member Betty Roberts was adopted. Hatfield supported the compromise decision.

On several other matters, Hatfield was unsuccessful in getting his desired policies through the legislature. Although he continued to push hard for the graduate research center in Portland and even gained a possible building for the proposed center, he could not win over the Salem politicians to his viewpoint. Home bases and loyalty to them counted more than Hatfield seemed to comprehend. Administrators at the University of Oregon and Oregon State University were reluctant to support the new center if it was not linked to their institutions but instead threatened competition to their in-place programs. Even less enthusiastic were Portland State supporters who thought their programs ought to be expanded first before public monies were used to fund a new facility. Hatfield failed to gain the legislators' support for his requested $600,000 to launch the graduate research center in Beaverton. Disappointed, the governor told one group of educators that "we need the research center and we will do it without legislative help and without public funds." It was not to be.

Other Hatfield agenda items met a similar fate. Although a proposed new state constitution was introduced, the legislative body adopted few of its suggested revisions. In fact, the revised version brought to the house and senate included so few notable changes that Hatfield thought it rather meaningless and said so. The revision attempts were dropped. So were his plans for an expanded base in tax policies, further reorganization of the state's executive branch, and a joining of the state's leading educational organizations, public schools and higher education, into an education committee.

While a large majority of Hatfield's energies were directed toward negotiations with and encouragements of the legislature, other attention was focused on emerging national and international events. One of these was the escalating conflict in Southeast Asia, in Vietnam. The governor had made his rather oblique criticism of Democrats' handling of this controversy in his keynote address at the Republican national convention the previous July, but in February 1965 he fired a broadside at Lyndon Johnson for his secrecy on Vietnam. The president needed to "give people the facts," the governor blasted. Americans should hear "the real purpose of a conflict which could involve us in another Asian war." Americans, Hatfield thought, might "want to stand firm in their support of the President," but they needed more "facts" and "information on which to base a stand." This arising tension between Hatfield and Johnson and the central government's war-making policies was adumbrative, foreshadowing a central position in his later senatorial career.

Even more extensive and widely reported was Hatfield's fiery reaction to the attempt of the Bureau of Land Management to exchange federally owned timber lands in southwestern Oregon for a private landowner's property in northern California to allow establishment of a national park. Hatfield exploded when he heard of this possible trade, which had been kept secret from him and other Oregon leaders for several months. Two facets of the clandestine agreement were particularly galling to the governor. The estimated value of the private land on the California coast north of the Bay Area had first been pegged at about $500,000, but just before the proposed switch the announced value jumped to about $2 million. Had the price on the coastal property been jacked up only when it was realized that the Oregon tract of federally owned forested land was given a $3 million price? Hatfield wondered. He was also upset that the federal government was making this decision without informing state officials or considering the economic impact of such a trade on Oregon. For several weeks, Oregon newspapers were filled with the governor's sharp criticisms of the Bureau of Land Management. Perhaps Hatfield's oppositional stance worked as he hoped; Secretary of the Interior Stewart Udall eventually withdrew the planned land switch.

The most unusual Hatfield connection with Washington, D.C., came through Antoinette rather than through the governor. While Oregon's first family was in the nation's capital to attend President Johnson's inauguration in January 1965, a television interviewer at the inaugural ball asked the governor's wife who she thought the Republican nominee in 1968 would be. Antoinette quickly replied, "I don't know, but whoever he is, he'll be better than what we have here tonight." After these offhand, from-the-hip words headlined several Oregon newspapers, legislator Beulah Hand, the talented but sharp-tongued Democrat from Milwaukie, introduced a memorial in the Oregon house attacking Mrs. Hatfield's comments and calling for an apology to the president. Hand, who seemed to enjoy pillorying Governor Hatfield for what she considered his weak leadership and excessive outside-Oregon travel, was now after his wife. The Hatfields did not respond to Representative Hand's comments, and later Antoinette stated that she did not make comments on political matters, even if they dealt with her husband. Perhaps the fiery reactions to her comments in early 1965 warned her away from political controversies. On the other hand, Beulah could castigate Antoinette's negative comments about the president as uncalled for and yet be guilty of the same kind of comments about the governor's wife.

The days following the legislative session were relatively quiet, allowing Hatfield respite and time for other matters. On several days in the January–May period, as many as six stories in a single issue of an Oregon newspaper dealt with

Hatfield's activities. From the beginning of June, things began to calm down, or so it seemed.

The calm was short-lived. By the end of July, Hatfield was back in the news. His explicit, forceful opposition to the Johnson administration's stance in Vietnam spiraled into newspaper headlines across the county, especially in Oregon. The outburst from Hatfield came at a national governors' conference in Minneapolis, where Vice-President Hubert Humphrey spoke and urged support for President Johnson's policies in Southeast Asia.

Extreme pressure was put on Hatfield, with nearly every governor at the gathering willing to support the president. But, following his controversial stance of the previous summer as the keynote speaker at the Republican national convention and well into the future, the Oregon governor expressed his strong opposition to the expanding U.S. role in Vietnam. Three years after the governors' convention, and in his first book, *Not Quite So Simple* (1968), Hatfield made clear his reasons for not supporting Lyndon B. Johnson. The president's policies were vague. What commitments was Johnson asking for? What were the president's ultimate goals in Vietnam? Were we right in thinking the deadly conflict in Vietnam was entirely a war against communist forces? After Hatfield voted no in the call to support the president's stand in Vietnam, Florida governor James Byrnes attacked Hatfield, telling television cameras and reporters, "What you [Hatfield] have done today is a disservice to your country." In the following months— and years—fellow evangelicals were also hard on Hatfield, denouncing him as not following biblical guidelines in supporting the president. Fallout from Hatfield's opposition to the Vietnam War continued several years into his senatorial career.

Hatfield's growing opposition to the Vietnam violence initiated a notable change in his relationship with Wayne

Morse, Oregon's senior senator. Less than eight years earlier, Morse, in a dramatic, last-minute attack had tried to derail Hatfield's run for governor by bringing up the tragic accident in which a car Hatfield was driving had killed a little girl. Now Morse was hailing Hatfield for his outspoken opposition to the Vietnam War, as noted by Morse's biographer, Mason Drukman: "Morse was supporting Hatfield for one reason: Hatfield was opposed to the war." Morse emphasized how much he and Hatfield had been able to work together on matters important to Oregon's present and future. Seeing Morse's willingness to compromise and bury bad feelings, Hatfield forged a new friendship. In the closing years of his role as governor, he and Morse were increasingly friendly. The support of the Democratic senator proved particularly beneficial for Hatfield in his run for the other Oregon senatorial seat in 1966.

Another controversial issue that captured Hatfield's attention in the summer and fall of 1965 was that concerning water policies and planning in the Pacific Northwest. Increasingly, the drier Southwest and California were casting covetous eyes on the Northwest's abundant water sources. As Hatfield put it, "Southern California is one thirsty camel whose nose we should let into our tent with the utmost caution." When Oregon and other Northwest leaders met to discuss the possibilities of water diversion, two views came quickly and clearly into focus. Some, like the newly elected governor of Washington, Dan Evans, and Idaho governor Robert Smylie were going to stiff-arm all attempts by southwesterners to gain water supplies from the Northwest. Others, like Hatfield, were more tentative, calling for additional meetings for discussion and planning. Once again illustrating his mediating positions on so many issues, Hatfield did not provide a yes-or-no answer to the water challenges. He wanted to wait and see—and then decide after more research and careful examinations.

But the governor was forced to speak out when other more political controversies surrounding water issues forced their way on to the scene. Beginning in the summer and stretching into the fall, Oregon state treasurer Robert Straub, a committed environmentalist, ambitious politician, and member of the influential Board of Control, leveled a series of attacks on Hatfield and his failures to deal with water and air pollution. In November, Straub blasted the governor, who he said had "shirked his responsibility to see that they [anti-pollution laws] are enforced." Hatfield had shown a "lack of leadership" in these needed areas. Intending to make a run for the governorship the next year, Straub did not let up in his criticism of Hatfield's handling of water and air pollution. One month later, veteran Hatfield opponent Beulah Hand launched another attack on the governor. Democratic state representative Hand pointed especially to Hatfield's failure to do something about mounting automobile emissions, which, she said, was still more evidence of the governor's lack of "intensive leadership."

Hatfield did not answer these specific charges. But he did present several ways in which these problems might be addressed. He called for, first of all, "water statesmanship" rather than "water politics." Statesmanship demanded careful planning among bordering states about the future of the Columbia River and the Columbia Basin. Similar study should come from within states wrestling with water supplies, uses of water, and the treatment of water sources (e.g., pollution problems). Not until thorough research and discussion had been carried out should states make important decisions about water allocation and treatment.

Hatfield was reluctant to move much beyond these regional and state efforts. True enough, federal government help might be needed, but it should not be invited on the scene until regional and statewide authorities carried out their needed research and planning.

Hatfield and the Oregon Board of Control. In the 1960s, the Board of Control was a powerful three-person executive group making important governing decisions. Here are Secretary of State Tom McCall, Governor Hatfield, and State Treasurer Bob Straub. Board of Control Records, Photographs and Drawings, Oversized, 88A-036/36/31. Oregon State Archives Division.

Hatfield's emphases on power at the state and local levels and his hesitation to open the door to federal policies and actions illustrate his links to Republican political views of the 1950s and 1960s. Since the huge expansion of federal government power in Franklin Roosevelt's New Deal policies of the 1930s, Republicans had urged voters to, first, pay attention to local freedoms and actions before embracing the overarching—and sometimes dominating—policies of a strong central government. The political stances of Robert A. Taft and Barry Goldwater were particularly illustrative of these Republican positions. And for Mark Hatfield, going back even further, the individualism and small-government

Republican ideology of Herbert Hoover played a central role in his thinking.

Hatfield's adherence to the Republican preferences for state-based over federal power and decision making showed up in several areas. Not only was he hesitant to encourage federal involvement in water source and pollution efforts, he also continued to stand against what he considered the wrongful actions of the Bureau of Land Management in trying to carry out measures harmful to Oregon forests and loggers. The same preference for state over federal control emerged in an address Hatfield gave at Oregon State University in mid-June. He told his young attendees that they must understand that more "personal involvement with less dependence on government" was necessary. At the governors' convention where Hatfield attacked the central government's policies in Vietnam, he also urged his fellow state executives "to develop a state-based national education policy aimed at heading off further federal intervention." Hatfield reiterated this view a few weeks later when he asserted that "the national interest can be better served by concerted state action than by monolithic federal action." In another quite different arena, Hatfield illustrated his preference for state-based control. In a controversy over Indian fishing rights, Hatfield rejected a Department of the Interior proposal to regulate those rights. States, not the federal government, should be in control. In these and other instances, Hatfield repeatedly made clear his preference for the Republican philosophy of local or state over federal direction.

Alongside Hatfield's support for Republican positions, he also repeated his convictions concerning the needed connections between one's religious-spiritual life and political stances. At the International Christian Leadership Conference in Seattle in early July, Hatfield met with noted evangelist Billy Graham and several other world Christian leaders. A week later Hatfield and other political and religious leaders gathered in Portland and issued an invitation to Graham to launch a future crusade there. Plus, at several governor's prayer breakfasts and in interviews with journalists, Hatfield presented his view that the religious beliefs of public officials should inform and shape their decisions. Yes, there should be a clear separation of church and state, but politicians had "the right to declare their religious convictions so long as they don't try to impose them on others." This close, sometimes nearly overlapping, relationship between one's religious beliefs and political leadership remained important to Hatfield throughout his long career.

While dealing with other challenges, Hatfield continued his energetic activities to encourage businesses already in Oregon and to woo dozens of others to the state. The most important of these in 1965 was an eighteen-day trip to Germany to further trade between that country and Oregon. The two Hatfields, two dozen Oregon businesspeople, their spouses, and a few journalists traveled to Germany. The trip included stops at a Volkswagen factory, a heavy machinery plant, other businesses, and even a brief visit with West Berlin mayor Willy Brandt and a short stop in East Berlin. Hatfield was entirely convinced the trip would enhance German-Oregon connections.

Not everything moved along smoothly in late 1965. Democrats railed against what they considered Hatfield's faulty leadership. Right-wing Republicans organized and put out publications attacking liberals like Hatfield. The new Job Corps center at Tongue Point, part of President Johnson's Great Society projects, experienced several disruptions, and Hatfield was even hanged in effigy by opponents protesting a change to Highway 101 near Pacific City on the coast.

But the Hatfields also experienced new blessings. Their fourth child, a second son named Charles Vincent after his two grandfathers, was born to the family in early October. Antoinette Hatfield received welcome salutes from Oregonians. In December, Oregon newspapers touted her roles

The Hatfield family. Hatfield was a devoted family man. He and Antoinette are seated here with their four children: Theresa (in Antoinette's lap, born 1964); Elizabeth (1959); Charles Vincent (Visko, in Mark's lap, 1965); and MarkO (1960). Image courtesy of Willamette University Archives and Special Collections.

as wife, mother, hostess, and author of a new recipe book. Author BJ in the *Oregonian* wrote, "With typical unobtrusive efficiency, Mrs. Mark O. Hatfield could have a baby in October, go to Europe a month later, return in December and have her Christmas gifts distributed the day after she returned home. The gifts are a collection of her favorite recipes in a Christmas red and white book, titled 'ReMARKable Recipes.'"

A large question hung over all these ideas and events: what would Hatfield do now? The Oregon constitution declared that he had but one year left as governor. Would the entrepreneurial governor go into business, as some speculated? Or might he become a college president since he had been offered such positions? Or would he, continuing his political journey of roughly fifteen years, take on Maurine Neuberger for her seat in the U.S. Senate? No one

139

was quite certain at the end of the year, and Hatfield had not given any substantive answers. 1966 lay ahead as a year of decision.

The announcement came in the second week of January—as usual in Silverton, Oregon. Mark Hatfield would run for the U.S. Senate in 1966. The announcement was no surprise. For two years—or more—voters and journalists alike had thought that Hatfield would, after completing his eight years in the governor's chair, compete with Maurine Neuberger for her senatorial seat.

Other surprises surrounded the notice, however. The largest wonders were the nonappearances of two possible Democratic opponents, incumbent Neuberger and Edith Green, both of whom chose not to rise up and take on Hatfield in the senatorial race. Publicly Neuberger claimed she planned to compete for reelection, but privately she confessed to her dissatisfaction of serving in the Senate and living in Washington. Plus, she had remarried a lawyer living in Boston, where she resided when not in Washington. By the end of 1965, Neuberger announced she would not enter the race.

The other strong Oregon Democrat, U.S. Representative Green, had gained considerable experience and seniority in her more than a decade representing Oregon's Third District. Some acquaintances, as well as the state's Democratic leaders, thought—and hoped—Green might be interested in gaining a seat in the Senate. But by early 1966 she had decided not to give up her seniority in the House to begin over again in the Senate.

The Democrats were in a quandary. Neither of their strong, experienced women wanted to run against Hatfield, the popular governor. Whom would they turn to now? Party leaders quickly pointed to Robert Duncan of Medford. A former member and speaker of the Oregon house and now in his second term in the U.S. House, Duncan had gained a dependable, strong reputation first as a lawyer and then as a politician. Plus, he had an added attraction: his pro-Vietnam stance and support for President Johnson in Southeast Asia would be the perfect foil for Hatfield's energetic and continuing opposition to the Vietnam War. Duncan could serve as the major point man in an area where Hatfield seemed the most vulnerable. Polls, informal and formal, indicated that most Oregonians generally supported Johnson in Vietnam, even if they had questions about vague, slippery parts of the president's policies. Now, Duncan, speaking for Oregon majorities, could go after the governor, particularly on Vietnam.

Just hours after Duncan announced his senatorial candidacy on 1 March, he began launching attacks on Hatfield's Vietnam stances. Those close to Duncan marveled at the changes that had taken place in their friend. Previously unknown for strongly worded criticism of persons and policies, he became a different man now in reacting to Mark Hatfield and Vietnam.

On 3 March, political columnist Harold E. Hughes quoted a string of Duncan's harsh criticisms of Hatfield. Duncan called to task those political leaders who could "destroy our effectiveness as a leader of the free world and its best hope for freedom and peace." Then, using words said to be Hatfield's, Duncan stated that he would not harpoon U.S. leaders for "terroristic or indiscriminate bombing" when, in fact, the U.S. military had carefully targeted only Viet Cong sites for its bombing. And then Duncan added what became one of his most-often quoted statements: "If we do not fight them in the 'elephant grass' [Hatfield's two words], we must fight in the pampas grass, and God help us, in the rye grass of our own state." Week after week, Duncan fired off similar broadsides at the governor, nearly all of which targeted Hatfield's stands on Vietnam.

The most unusual part of Duncan's comments is that he was not yet an opponent of Hatfield's. That opposition would come only if Duncan won the Democratic and Hatfield the Republican primary; then they would face off for the November election. Meanwhile, Duncan faced a worthy opponent in his own party, Howard Morgan, for the May primary. And in attacking Hatfield on Vietnam, Duncan was also firing at Morgan. A former chairman of Oregon's Democratic Party and a power commissioner at the Oregon and national levels, Morgan was a well-known, outspoken man, particularly in his opposition to American policies in Vietnam.

Meanwhile, Hatfield's statements on Vietnam changed little over time, even though his critics asserted that they had. Since his first vague references to Vietnam in his keynote address in 1965 and through antiwar comments at several governors' conferences and Republican gatherings, Hatfield had made his position clear. About two weeks after announcing his candidacy for the Senate, Hatfield told the Press Club in Phoenix, Arizona, that President Johnson's policies in Vietnam were "a colossal failure." For Hatfield, the president had not made his policies understandable, had failed to invite the United Nations to help sponsor peace efforts, and had not gained support from other free nations. Moreover, free speech on the controversy was limited because those who criticized were labeled unpatriotic or "soft on communism."

Democrats, including Duncan, painted Hatfield not as a "hawk" (for the war) or as a "dove" (against the war) but as a "duck," one dodging reality and often ducking away to a new, different position. These opponents missed some of the complexity of Hatfield's stances. True enough, he stood for political support of American troops fighting in Vietnam while, simultaneously, opposing the war there. That was an example of his "ducking" or "mugwumping" actions, according to his opponents. But they failed to—or chose not to—see the distinctions Hatfield was making. In fact, more than a century earlier Abraham Lincoln had made a similar distinction and was condemned for his "wiggle-waggles." Lincoln harshly criticized President James K. Polk for launching the Mexican-American War—dismissing it as "Polk's war"—but at the same time he supported all legislative backing for the troops. For Mark Hatfield, as for Abraham Lincoln, supporting fighting forces on the field while opposing what he considered a wrongful war was not political waffling. Hatfield did not change his opposition to the Vietnam War—through the primary vote in May and on to the final election in November. But he did add other planks to his stance on the war, as we shall see.

Hatfield had minor competition in his primary run for the Republicans. Walter Huss, a conservative Republican and fundamentalist minister, won 30,906 votes; Jim Bacaloff, 19,699; and frequent candidate George Altvater, 6,155. Hatfield received about 75 percent of the Republican vote, 175,782. He had not campaigned energetically, perhaps saving his time for the serious, more competitive run in the fall.

Democrats thought Howard Morgan would give Robert Duncan a close race. That prediction proved wrong. Duncan outpolled Morgan 161,189 to 89,174. A third candidate, Gilbert Meyers, received only 8,783 votes.

By the end of June, the Hatfield-Duncan race was already warming up. The first polls of summer indicated a slight Duncan lead. To win he must retain Democratic voters, who outnumbered Republicans by 110,000. Also, other polls suggested that about three out of four Oregonians favored Lyndon Johnson's policies. These figures revealed that at least two major challenges faced Hatfield if he was to win a seat in the Senate: he had to win over pro-Vietnam supporters in spite of his antiwar position; he must also attract thousands of crossover Democratic voters to his Republican candidacy. It would be a demanding, time-consuming battle.

During the summer, Hatfield traveled the campaign trail more than Duncan, whose time in Oregon was lessened because he had to maintain his presence in Washington, D.C., when U.S. House affairs called for his participation. Many of Hatfield's foes continued to label him a "duck," asserting that the governor dodged back and forth and repeatedly changed his positions on Vietnam. These criticisms, for the most part, were based more on partisan politics than on political facts. Hatfield continued his central positions on Vietnam: he opposed American presence there because he viewed the conflict as a nationalistic conflict rather than primarily a controversy between western style democracy and communism; he continued to support American soldiers in the war; and he provided a string of suggestions on how the conflict might be ended. These maneuvers, if carried out, could keep the Vietnam conflict from descending into a horrendous, long-lasting land war over Indochina.

The list of suggestions never included a quick pullout. That precipitous move, Hatfield was convinced, was dangerous in every way. Instead, he suggested other steps. Hatfield thought President Johnson's leadership especially flawed in failing to bring the United Nations into the controversy and asking U.S. allies to become involved. Increasingly, Hatfield called for an All-Asia Conference to discuss Vietnam. He was particularly pleased when such a conference was convened in Manila, although it did not accomplish much on Vietnam. The Johnson administration had failed to state clearly U.S. objectives in Vietnam; the government leaders must do that. Finally, the escalating costs of the Asian war were disrupting the American economy; for that reason alone, the Vietnam policies needed to change.

Throughout the summer Hatfield pushed hard on the need for policy shifts in Vietnam. But his anti-Vietnam stance was unpopular. When he attended a governors' conference in early July, he was outvoted forty-nine to one in speaking out against President Johnson's actions in Vietnam. In Oregon alone it was estimated that 75 percent of residents supported the war; even some of Hatfield's Republicans in the state did not back his position on the war.

From the primary on, Vietnam was *the* campaign issue between Hatfield and Duncan. The Democratic candidate, sensing that Hatfield's stance was unpopular, pounded away on the governor's position. Then, in September, emphases began to shift. Whether Hatfield decided to make the change, whether his advisors suggested he do so, or whether both were at work, Hatfield began to "break free" from the sole emphasis on Vietnam.

Hatfield did not abandon the war, but he linked it to other issues important to Oregonians. When it became clear that his chances for winning the senatorial race were lessened when he spoke only of his strong opposition to the Vietnam War, he began to widen the issues on which he campaigned. Chief among these new emphases was the nation's economy, particularly what he considered the fouled-up economic policies of the Johnson administration. As a fiscal conservative, Hatfield found abundant grounds to point to Johnson's war as a major cause of rising inflation and tighter money. He blasted the escalating military costs as a reason for economic problems. He also pointed to foreign aid expenditures as excessive. The governor showed another side of his political philosophy and actions when he attacked the president's Great Society as far too expensive and yet accepted the Job Corps sites and called for federal funds to help with welfare issues. The key to these shifts was that Hatfield was still speaking against the Vietnam War, but now he was linking that problem to the country's rising economic woes.

In the days stretching from the end of the May primary to September, most political polls listed Duncan slightly ahead in an otherwise very close election. Then the numbers began to shift as Hatfield went full tilt on the campaign trail, preaching different kinds of messages. The governor urged voters to push for peace in Vietnam, to oppose President Johnson's huge expenditures and flawed leadership, and to keep their eyes, first of all, on Oregon needs rather than so much on foreign matters. The Hatfield campaign, profiting from mounting contributions, launched a deluge of newspaper and television advertisements from September to November.

Plus, Hatfield himself galloped throughout the state on a series of tiring and yet exhilarating campaign trips. For example, in early October he traveled to eastern Oregon on a five-day trip, visiting towns such as Burns, Vale, and Ontario. He made numerous presentations, speaking to student and town groups, delivering luncheon and dinner addresses, and walking into supermarkets to shake hands. He addressed the need for tax reform since voters had hoped for but failed to get an initiative measure on the fall ballot. He also urged eastern Oregonians to push for diplomacy rather than heightened military action in Vietnam. Finally, he made sure to mention the difficulties farmers and lumbering industries were facing in the state and that he supported legislation to help these faltering occupations.

Robert Duncan, meanwhile, was unable to match Hatfield's vigorous campaigning. House of Representative duties, family needs of seven children, Medford residence, and less bountiful contributions from Democratic supporters added to the difficulties of Duncan's campaign. Plus, his attacks on Hatfield's anti-Vietnam stances worked well during the summer but seemed to lose steam as fall came on. Pollsters were still speaking of a toss-up or dead-heat senatorial run, but most of the polls were now giving Hatfield the slightest edge in projected numbers.

The campaign sparked several intriguing outcomes. One of the most memorable was Senator Wayne Morse's position on Hatfield. Recall that Morse tried to undermine Hatfield's run for governor in 1958. By 1966 relations between the senator and the governor had changed; they were talking and even working together on measures such as the Boardman project, the proposed industrial and military development in eastern Oregon near the Columbia River. And when Hatfield spoke out against the war in Vietnam, Morse congratulated him for the same position the senior senator had already taken nationally. Democrat Morse went one step farther in promising to support Republican Hatfield in the junior senatorial race when fellow Democrat Duncan came out in support of the war. Morse did speak out for Hatfield, although he did not agree with the governor in all areas concerning the Southeast Asia war.

Toward the end of the campaign, the Duncan-Hatfield race, particularly Hatfield's role in it, gathered a good deal of national attention. In their splashy covers, *Time* and *Newsweek* featured Hatfield and others involved in close runs for national office. National columnist Tom Wicker predicted Hatfield would win because the governor was so well known and much loved in Oregon. Several national television programs also featured brief stories on Hatfield.

Into the fall, Hatfield's star was clearly on the rise. Campaign funds poured in, totaling eventually about $330,000, the most expensive campaign thus far in Oregon's history. On 6 November, two days before the election, the *Oregonian* warmly endorsed Hatfield on its editorial page. The editor noted that in his sixteen years in public office Hatfield had "explored and acted on every phase of economic and social activity of the people." He had "sold" Oregon to tourists, brought in new industries, and become "the state's best-known citizen not only in his own state but nationally." His support of industrial expansion and recreational activities and places, along with his religious faith, marked him "as a statesman." In short, the writer concluded, Oregon could not "afford to pass up this opportunity to send the nation's finest young governor to the United States Senate." On the same day, a full-page advertisement supporting Hatfield carried thousands of names and the endorsements of more than twenty Oregon newspapers.

Those who predicted a close election and a narrow win for Hatfield were exactly right. Hatfield polled 348,391 votes to Duncan's 325,810. Duncan had done well in Portland and other strong Democratic areas, but Hatfield was stronger throughout the state. Some thought Hatfield had done especially well because 1966 was a "Republican year" throughout the country, allowing actor Ronald Reagan to upset incumbent Pat Brown as governor in California, electing Tom McCall to the Oregon governor's chair to replace Hatfield, and providing a solid Republican majority in the looming 1967 legislature. Others pointed in other directions. One Oregon newspaper posited that Hatfield "polished the smoothest, most efficiently run political machine seen in modern times in Oregon." Still another source, *Newsweek,* argued that "postelection analysis shows that it was Hatfield's name, good looks and Statehouse record that really won for him." However one viewed the outcome, Mark Hatfield had won an election by nearly 25,000 votes over a worthy opponent. Now he was headed for the U.S. Senate.

True to form, just a few hours after his victory Mark Hatfield, accompanied by Antoinette, flew east to make several speeches and to plan the future. While in the nation's capital, the Hatfields rented a house in Bethesda, Maryland, close to the children's school and about a half hour from the Senate building. Not quite close enough for Mark to come home for lunch, the Hatfields chuckled. Leolyn Barnett, secretary for twenty years for Oregon governors including most recently Hatfield, would move to Washington and become the new senator's secretary. Warne Nunn, another longtime Hatfield aide, would also join his boss in Washington.

In the hectic weeks of late November and the month of December, Hatfield tried to tie together loose ends of state politics and prepare his family for their move across the country. As required by Oregon's constitution, Hatfield prepared a budget for the 1967 legislature, even though he would not be dealing with it. A huge projection of more than $600 million, the budget nonetheless thoroughly cut much larger requests from state agencies. As usual, the educational figures made up fully half of the total request. After filing the budget, Hatfield made little comment on it, allowing such reactions to come from new governor Tom McCall and members of the legislature.

The number of Hatfield's talks diminished after his election to the Senate, but the focus of the presentations remained much the same. At the December graduation ceremony at Pacific University, the governor strongly criticized U.S. foreign policy, calling into question its leaders, thinking, and actions. The country's values were shoddy, based on unclear thinking, wrongheaded, or vague in goal setting. For example, in Vietnam, Asians should take over the fighting since, obviously, it was an Asian not an American war. More positively, Hatfield touted his eight-year governorship as moving "Oregon out of the economic doldrums with industrial and economic development." He made sure an interviewer also heard that during his administration seven hundred industrial plants were either begun or expanded, bringing in 180,000 new jobs. Hatfield thought, too, that under his leadership the political tone in Oregon had been transformed, away from the excessively conservative and toward the more moderate and less contentious.

In his final message sent to the legislature, Hatfield summarized what he saw as his achievements but also called for additional moves to strengthen the state. He pointed to his being only the second Oregon governor to complete two four-year terms (and the only one in the twentieth century) and asserted that during those years Oregonians experienced the "period of the greatest economic expansion in the state's history." He also mentioned the completion of Interstate 5 from California to Washington, the erection of the long bridge across the mouth of the Columbia River at Astoria, and the increased automobile safety throughout the state's highways as important achievements. The governor was convinced, however, that much more needed to be done to protect Oregon's water sources, avoid pollution-producing businesses, and sustain the state's lagging logging industry. Finally, once again Hatfield called for the net receipts tax policy that would bring all citizens under the tax umbrella, even at the beginning levels, so as to reduce the taxes of homeowners. After Hatfield delivered parts of this letter during his in-person farewell message, incoming Governor McCall followed, saying of Hatfield that "no other man has left his 'imprint on so many state actions, policies and programs.'"

In the closing days of Hatfield's governorship, vague projections were made about his forthcoming roles as a new senator. Most of all, he was viewed as an outspoken opponent of President Johnson's Vietnam policies as well as against what he saw as the president's dominating uses of federal power to rule over states. Most thought Hatfield would be an outstanding, vigorous proponent of policies helpful to Oregon.

The final hours and immediate aftermath of Hatfield's governorship were action-packed. After presenting his farewell message on the morning of 9 January, Hatfield hustled to the airport to fly to Washington, D.C. On the next day, he was sworn in to the U.S. Senate. A new era lasting thirty years had begun.

5

From Salem to Washington, D.C.—and Beyond

In early 1967, Mark Hatfield plummeted from the Mount Hood apex of Oregon politics to the bottom of the U.S. Senate in Washington, D.C. If his Lincoln Town Car license of No. 1 symbolized his pinnacle of political power as Oregon's governor, his ranking of 100 in the Senate indicated he was at the opposite end, at the bottom, and the beginning place of that august group. Hatfield would have to start all over again—now on the national scene.

The first months—and even initial years—of Hatfield's political journey in the nation's capital featured his learning lessons and making adjustments. The largest adjustment, of course, was reverting back to a legislative position from his decade as an executive as Oregon's secretary of state and governor. Now he was again a legislator. As Hatfield himself put it, "There were plenty of rough parts to my transition."

Some of the transitional challenges were low key and short-lived. At the foot of the totem pole, new senators ended up with offices near the back alley or in a newly abandoned closet. Hatfield had to face some of these indignities in his first months in Washington.

Much more significant were the changes a freshman senator faced in the seniority system of the Senate. He had to wait his turn at the end of the line when attempting to speak to an issue on the Senate floor. He had to give way to senior senators in areas of prestige, assignments, and even listings. One of the major challenges was in committee assignments. A newcomer could request selection for a much-favored committee, but he or she rarely won out in the selection process. Hatfield was more fortunate in some ways, because the Republicans had done so well in 1966 and were attempting to flex their committee muscles in early 1967. Hatfield won a seat on his desired Senate Interior Committee and was also named to Agricultural and Forestry and Small Business committees, all groups that Hatfield had had considerable experience with and on which he wished to serve.

Another transitional challenge came in making new connections with senatorial colleagues. Hatfield arrived with no close senatorial friends other than Wayne Morse, but he soon began working with other senators who shared his views on key issues. Democrat George McGovern and Hatfield, for example, worked across party lines to introduce anti–Vietnam War legislation. Hatfield connected with Democratic senator Harold Hughes of Iowa, sharing evangelical experiences in lunches and prayer breakfasts.

Not all the transitions from Oregon governor to U.S. senator were those of change; continuities also shaped Hatfield's first term in Congress. As we shall see, the carryover of opposition to the Vietnam War was a major view that persisted. Oregon issues facing Hatfield the governor became part of the agenda of Hatfield the senator when his maiden speech in the Senate dealt with logging issues in Oregon and what should be done about the troubled industry. Hundreds of letters continued to flow into the new senator's office dealing with water, welfare, highway, and other economic, social, and political issues. The senator had to keep up with these contacts, as he had as governor.

A bit more than a year after Hatfield arrived in the Senate, he faced perhaps the most momentous "what-if" of his political career: the election of 1968 and Hatfield's

Mark Hatfield and Richard Nixon. Hatfield and Nixon became friends in the 1950s. Later the Hatfield and Nixon couples met socially on a few occasions. Photo courtesy of the *Oregonian*.

nearly becoming the Republican vice president on the presidential ticket of Richard Nixon. Hatfield and Nixon had been acquaintances, especially since the Oregon governor supported Nixon in his unsuccessful run against John F. Kennedy in 1960. Hatfield also remained much closer to Nixon's political stances than those of Barry Goldwater, even though he supported the Arizona senator for president in 1964. Political advisors saw much in Hatfield's youthfulness, vigor, and popularity that could add to Nixon's ticket in 1968.

As Republican leaders immediately began planning for the party's full ticket after Nixon won the presidential nomination on 8 August in Miami Beach, several spoke of Hatfield as a possible vice-presidential candidate. Others had hesitations: they thought Hatfield was too controversial in his opposition to the Vietnam War; he was too close geographically to Nixon the Californian; and as a supporter of civil rights he had no pull with southerners, a segment of the voting public the Nixonites were pursuing in their "southern strategy." Still, news stories repeatedly named Hatfield as one running mate Nixon was considering.

Rumors put Hatfield in the top small group being considered for vice president. In fact, one Miami newspaper precipitously—and wrongly—blazoned an afternoon edition with the headline "Nixon and Hatfield." The Hatfields, tired of all the frenzy, went to bed with the veep position still to be decided. Evangelist Billy Graham, a friend of Nixon and Hatfield and supporting the new Oregon senator for vice president, called Hatfield early the next morning to tell him that he was still in the running. A bit later Graham called again to say, no, another person had been chosen. Not until the Hatfields came down the next morning did they hear that Spiro Agnew, the conservative governor of Maryland, had been selected as Nixon's running mate. When one recalls that in the future Agnew was thrown out of office and that Nixon was forced to resign on the threat

Hatfield and Billy Graham. Dedicated evangelicals, Hatfield and Graham became close friends. Graham pushed hard, but unsuccessfully, for Hatfield as vice president in 1968. Photo courtesy of Billy Graham Evangelistic Association.

of impeachment, that means Mark Hatfield, if he had been selected for vice president in 1968, may well have become U.S. president in summer 1974.

Hatfield was conflicted in his reactions to not winning the nomination. He would have welcomed the opportunity to march to a win with Nixon, but he also realized that his views on Vietnam and other matters were so much at variance with Nixon's that White House harmony might have disappeared. Hatfield wondered, too, if he could have remained a devoted husband and father if he had become vice president.

The major and most time-consuming issues of Hatfield's first term as a senator involved the Vietnam War. Hatfield carried into the Senate from Oregon his strong opposition to the war, and that opposition dominated much of his political life until a peace treaty was signed in 1973 and South Vietnam fell in 1975.

In numerous speeches, essays, and *Not Quite So Simple,* Hatfield outlined his major reasons for standing against the war. In fact, half of his book thoroughly addresses the history of Vietnam leading up to the U.S. involvement in the 1960s, President Johnson's flawed leadership in dealing with Vietnam, and what Hatfield thought should be done to end the war. Over time, Hatfield summarized his opinions on the Vietnam War in several succinct points: (1) American leaders and many voters failed—or chose not to see—the Vietnam conflict as primarily a civil war of nationalism, and not one of communism versus freedom; (2) President Johnson had lied when he promised not to send soldiers to fight in Vietnam (that was just one of a series of Johnson's leadership failures); (3) the war was killing off tens of thousands of Vietnamese people, not saving them from destruction, as we had vowed; (4) the war was based on several wrongheaded theories, including the "domino theory" that posited that the loss of Vietnam would inevitably lead to a series of losses in Asia and that defeating North Vietnam would hold off the aggressive expansionism of China; (5) American leaders should work with our allies and the United Nations to find peace in Southeast Asia; and, finally, (6) Hatfield would continue to support soldiers in the battles even while he opposed the war.

Once in the Senate, Hatfield moved in antiwar directions not typical of a state's governor. In late 1967 and early 1968, he introduced a resolution to limit the Vietnam War to Vietnam, keeping it from expanding into Cambodia and elsewhere, and to allow the president's war decisions to go into effect only after Congress gave its permission. The resolution did not gain much support. In fall 1970, Hatfield and Senator Frank Church of Idaho introduced a bill to speed up troop withdrawal. It lost. Most significant were a series of antiwar measures Hatfield and Democrat George McGovern drafted in the early 1970s. Especially important was legislation limiting funding for future troop buildups and eventually moving toward ending the war itself. The McGovern-Hatfield measure won the support of other senators such as Harold Hughes, Church, and Charles Goodell. First, the bill got 39 votes and later 49. National events in 1972–74 usually sidelined additional measures of this kind.

These actions transformed Mark Hatfield into a nationally recognized antiwar or peace leader. His office often received one hundred or more letters daily, most of them positive, about Hatfield's opposition to the war. Such was Hatfield's recognition that there was talk in 1972 that he might run on a bipartisan peace ticket with Democrat Eugene McCarthy, or, behind the scenes, join George McGovern's campaign as his vice-presidential candidate. Another small group encouraged him to run for the presidency on a peace platform.

Unfortunately for Hatfield, the fallout from his antiwar stances among fellow Christians was often negative and emotionally draining. One believer, upset with Hatfield's voiced opposition to the war, wrote of his now-disbelieving view of the senator: he was "a former brother in Christ." Others

Senator George McGovern. Hatfield and McGovern, both with evangelical backgrounds, were strong antiwar advocates in the U.S. Senate. There was some talk of a McGovern (D) and Hatfield (R) ticket in 1972. Courtesy Library of Congress, LC-DIG-ppmsca-19602 (digital file).

called attention to the biblical admonition in Romans 13 that believers were to "be subject to the governing authorities"; those who did not follow their leaders were resisting God since they were God-appointed; resisters would "incur judgment." Still others questioned Hatfield's faith. One letter writer noted that he had heard Hatfield speak of his belief in "Jesus Christ as your personal savior," but because he would not "support the boys in Vietnam and . . . [was] fighting President Nixon who had been placed there by God," this writer knew that Hatfield was not a follower of Christ. Hatfield testified to how hard the dismissive reactions of evangelicals hit him. At the end of 1971 he was seriously thinking of not running for reelection.

Still other events and reactions buoyed Hatfield's spirits. One he and his biographers all mention was his invitation to give the commencement address at the powerhouse Fuller

Seminary in Pasadena, California, in June 1970. Hatfield faced the appearance with trepidation since campus riots on Southeast Asia issues had exploded on dozens of college campuses the previous weeks. But just as Hatfield walked toward the podium with the seminary president, students enthusiastically unrolled a banner with the words "We're with you, Mark." He also received a message that dozens of the seminary faculty members supported his antiwar stances—as well as his upstanding role as a leading evangelical. Such positive reinforcements as the one at Fuller revived Hatfield's faltering spirits and turned him around for another run at the Senate.

While divisive reactions to the Vietnam War were exploding across the United States from D.C. to the West Coast, a new political trend was under way in Oregon. It had begun with the Republican win of Hatfield for the Senate and Tom McCall for governor in 1966. It continued in 1968 when upstart Republican state legislator Robert Packwood upset Wayne Morse in a run for the U.S. Senate. Now in 1972, Morse was anxious to get back in the Senate. The mercurial Morse had earlier switched from Republican, to independent, and then to Democrat affiliation. But in Hatfield's win over Duncan in 1966, Morse had crossed party lines to support Hatfield because of his anti-Vietnam stance. Now, Morse, once again changing, was coming back to run against Hatfield.

In reporting on the Hatfield-Morse campaign, the *New York Times* concluded that it "lacked the heated debate because voters apparently saw little difference between the two candidates"—true enough in that both were seen as liberals, and both opposed the Vietnam War. But Morse saw differences; they "are legion," the Democrat asserted. He thought Hatfield followed Richard Nixon "too closely." Voters seemed to see and follow other differences. Morse was seventy-two years old, Hatfield fifty. Hatfield campaigned more vigorously, even though he was tied to a senatorial schedule and Morse wasn't. Morse loved to attack, but Hatfield responded that even though he disagreed with President Nixon he had "never attacked him personally." The *Oregonian,* not much excited about either candidate, nonetheless came out for Hatfield. Plus, the Nixon presidential win in Oregon by nearly 10 percent over Democrat George McGovern undoubtedly helped swing the election for Hatfield. When the results came in, it was clear the election was not as close as some predicted; Hatfield bested Morse by a 494,671 (53.7 percent) to 425,036 (46.2 percent) margin.

In early 1973, Hatfield returned to the Senate with bits of seniority and more recognition. He would now face major issues quite different from those in his first senatorial term.

On 27 January 1973, the Paris Peace Treaty ended the Vietnam War for the United States. Although the Senate did not ratify the treaty and North and South Vietnam continued their fighting for more than two years, the United States had terminated its involvement in the unfortunate, unsuccessful campaign. That meant Capitol Hill was no longer tied up with this divisive issue from 1973 onward as it had been in Mark Hatfield's first years in the Senate.

Although the Vietnam War virtually disappeared from Hatfield's senatorial agenda, other subjects linked to the war gained his notice. One of the war-related issues was the draft, which Hatfield thought particularly unfair. While students and scions of upper classes often sought and obtained deferment, lower-income sons were being drafted and bearing the brunt of wars. From 1967 to 1970, Hatfield introduced bills to end the draft; none passed, but after growing antidraft support Nixon ended conscription in 1973. Second, the Oregon senator also supported amnesty for those who resisted and evaded the draft in a "principled" manner. In a coauthored book, *Amnesty?* (1973), he backed amnesty because that measure had been a policy the United

States followed in previous wars. Third, Hatfield sought to have prisoners of war (POWs) released and information gathered on those still missing in action. He hoped these actions would help keep peace and ward off mistaken future actions like the Vietnam debacle.

Once Hatfield failed in 1968 to gain the nomination for the vice presidency, his relations with newly elected president Nixon moved in other directions beginning in 1969. When Hatfield criticized Nixon's actions in Vietnam and chose not to support other presidential measures, the gap widened—so much so that a few years later Hatfield was placed on the "enemies list" at the White House.

Hatfield and Nixon had gradually separated even before the first rumors surfaced of the president's wrongful actions in the election of 1972. When the frenzy over Watergate escalated during the next two years, leading to Nixon's resignation in August 1974, Hatfield remained relatively quiet. Some thought Hatfield's silence came about because, out of party loyalty, he did not want the Watergate upheaval to inordinately damage his Republican Party. Others stated that Hatfield did not say much because he wanted to refrain from attacking Nixon personally. Still others noted that Hatfield, though he could be counted on to speak his conscience, was cautious about coming to quick conclusions that would rattle others.

Hatfield did make a few illuminating comments, however, that later cast light on his Watergate reactions. On 1 February 1973, he spoke at the annual national prayer breakfast, warning an audience of nearly three thousand that adhering to a "civil religion" uniting religion and politics rather than relying on the biblical teachings of Jesus was a dangerous path. Wrongly following a civil religion helped lead, Hatfield said in referring to the Vietnam War, to "the sin that scarred our national soul." "We must turn in repentance" from such actions. As Hatfield made these comments, President Nixon and his wife sat to the speaker's right; to his left, evangelist Billy Graham. The evangelist was so embarrassed with Hatfield's comments that he wrote the senator a letter requesting that he send an apology to the president.

As additional information on Watergate continued to emerge, the breaking news of Vice President Spiro Agnew's criminal activities added to the upheaval. Hearing about Agnew's misdeeds, Hatfield told a news network, "We have a period of time when there is political erosion. Confidence and faith in the whole system has been challenged by many people. And now to have this kind of confirmation of the worst suspicions that some people have held is really a very profound impact on the whole country."

As the Watergate story expanded and began sneaking in the front door of the White House, Hatfield, increasingly upset with these happenings, called for a national day of humiliation, fasting, and prayer in April 1974. Influenced in this action by Abraham Lincoln's similar call more than a century earlier, Hatfield asked all Americans "to confess and repent of national sins." The U.S. Senate passed the resolution by a voice vote, but it was never approved in the House. Increasing numbers of churches and other groups supported the idea, but columnist Art Buchwald labeled the idea "The Day We All Eat Humble Pie."

By early summer 1974, with Nixon's impeachment seeming more and more imminent, Hatfield was less reluctant to speak out on Watergate. "It seems to me," he told a radio interviewer, "the President is almost intent on committing political hara-kiri." The Oregon senator hoped "we can resolve this short of impeachment" but added that Nixon's action "invites far more serious consideration" as events moved along. Although Hatfield served on the Senate Rules Committee, which was in charge of the guidelines surrounding impeachment, he and his committee members were saved from that activity when Nixon resigned in August 1974.

Even as the unfolding events of the Watergate scandal upset Washington, Hatfield was moving in other directions. During his second stint in the Senate, his thinking and writing turned more and more to his Christian outlook and how that way of thinking should be adapted to politics and the world's basic needs. Hatfield, of course, was interested in the relationships between his evangelical point of view and American politics and welfare needs well before his senatorial career began, but the earlier interests were much as a sideshow compared to the big-tent perspective Hatfield launched while serving in the Senate.

Some think this enlarged view came from a group of young evangelicals Hatfield met after becoming a senator. These young men remained his friends; some even came to work as staff members in his Senate office. Hatfield biographers also point to the senator's enormous book collection and his tireless reading as sources for his enlarged thinking on the political and social side of what they termed Hatfield's "progressive evangelism." This expanding thinking involving a Christian outlook on politics and social needs is particularly evident in Hatfield's book *Between the Rock and the Hard Place* (1976), written during his second term as a senator.

A central question emerged from Hatfield's book: what was to be the Christian leader's or follower's role in American society? Carefully searching the preachments of Old Testament prophets and Jesus Christ in the New Testament, Hatfield was convinced the role was certainly not one of power and privilege. Instead, modern disciples of Christ must become servants, giving away their lives in service for the good of American society as well as the world as a whole. Though Hatfield had voiced this message beforehand, it increasingly became his central guideline—first for himself and then for other leaders.

Hatfield realized, of course, that several barriers lay before anyone trying to implement the Christian guidelines he now embraced. The American political system, as followed in the 1970s, was a huge obstacle facing the Christian idealist wanting political reform. In an unusually metaphorical and negative statement, Hatfield blasted the prevailing American political system: "A façade of statesman idealism conceals a brothel of egomania and lust for power which prostitute those in political life for often nothing more than personal vainglory." Further, as Hatfield pointed out elsewhere, another huge barrier existed *among* Christians: "There is a theological 'silent majority' in our land," he noted pointedly about right-wing believers he called Fundamentalists, "who wrap their Bibles in the American flag, who believe that conservative politics is the necessary by-product of orthodox Christianity; who equate patriotism with the belief in national self-righteousness; and who regard political dissent as a mark of infidelity to the faith." Hatfield himself had been the target of the latter groups when they attacked him for his opposition to the Vietnam War.

Something had to be done to reform the American political system, and Hatfield, now more than ever driven by his Christian ethic, began to introduce a series of legislative measures that would bring about needed change. Among the most prominent, (1) repeal the draft law; (2) amend the Constitution so as to hold separate elections for the president, vice president, and some cabinet members; (3) redirect up to 80 percent of a person's taxes to local concerns, thereby reducing federal control; (4) establish term limits for top officeholders; and (5) simplify tax forms to give individuals and small businesses more control over their livelihood. Hatfield realized that some of these proposals would never be passed—and most were not—but he also was convinced that they were necessary to make American politics more humane, less powerful at the core, and more responsive to citizens.

Hatfield's enlarged commitment to the "relational dimension of faith" also spilled over into worldwide social welfare challenges. He had been negatively labeled a "new isolationist" as a foe of the Vietnam War, but now he was becoming freshly viewed as a man who wanted to look after the entire globe. For this challenging, needy world, he also had idealistic goals. In the closing chapter of *Between a Rock and a Hard Place,* Hatfield advances several ideas, especially ones focusing on poverty and hunger. Americans, especially Christian Americans, had to begin with a clearer and more comprehensive view of biblical teachings. Jesus spoke extensively about poverty and the need of believers to help the poor. He related the Good Samaritan story and urged others to aid the needy. He also pointed out how much the hungry and powerless needed help. Applying these principles to the 1970s, Hatfield urged readers and listeners to do the following: reduce excessive military expenditures; be more disciplined in their food consumption; never accept the poverty, injustices, hunger, and other needs of others; look for ways to help with an ethic of love; and, finally, organize national, community and church, and individual groups to address these worldwide needs.

Hatfield's commitment to aid the global poor and hungry expanded a level or two when he met famed religious servant Mother Teresa. Hatfield, Antoinette, and their two oldest children, Elizabeth and MarkO, traveled to India and visited Mother Teresa in her expansive compound in Calcutta. The Hatfields saw the nun's diligent and sustaining labors with the poor, orphans, the hungry and sick, and the dying. Seeing Mother Teresa endlessly working with the world's broken greatly impacted Hatfield. "This visit with Mother Teresa, the woman, the saint," he wrote, "provided me with one of the greatest highlights of my life."

As 1978 opened and Hatfield faced another election, his political situation in Oregon proved to be much different than it was in 1966 and 1972 in his first two elections to the Senate. No one came forward with the political backing that Robert Duncan and Wayne Morse brought to those two rather taxing runs. Vernon Cook, an Oregon state legislator from Gresham, won the spring Democratic primary handily without much competition, as did Hatfield with equal ease in the Republican primary. Cook was an energetic campaigner and often criticized Hatfield, but he failed to gain traction in the election. Plus, with abundant funding, Hatfield greatly outspent his Democratic opponent. Pollsters were right in predicting an easy Hatfield win. Hatfield rolled up 550,615 (61.7 percent) votes to Cook's 341,616 (38.3 percent). Although Democrats far outnumbered registered Republicans, Hatfield had easily won his third election to the Senate.

Only later did most political historians realize how Mark Hatfield was increasingly falling from the pinnacle of notoriety that he gained in 1968 when he came within a whisker of becoming the vice president. In the late 1970s and afterward, Hatfield was no longer touted as a young, possible presidential or vice-presidential candidate. Although only age fifty-six when he began his third term as senator, Hatfield had been passed by at the top. But in another way he was on his way up, having served twelve years and now gaining more senior status. His voice would be heard, his words read in increasing numbers of national political debates.

One key for understanding Hatfield's senatorial role in the late 1970s is through his complex relationships with presidents Jimmy Carter and Ronald Reagan. Neither of these relationships was entirely positive or negative; both reveal a good deal about Senator Hatfield.

One would think that Mark Hatfield and Jimmy Carter might have become fast friends. They had much in common: committed, lifetime evangelicals (Baptists) from strong families; servicemen; loyal husbands and devoted fathers; ambitious, self-driven young men; former governors. These commonalities did lead to some connections. Before Carter became president in 1977, Hatfield had been in the Senate for a decade, and Carter evidently knew of him. In his *White House Diary*, Carter wrote, "Mark Hatfield was a kind of hero of mine. . . . I was filled with admiration for him." Carter also joined and participated in a Senate prayer group, which Hatfield attended. Other similarities came into focus. Both men opposed abortion on demand and agreed that the Panama Canal ought to be returned to Panama's control.

But the differences between the two admirable evangelical politicians also kept them apart. First the separation of competing political parties: Carter a lifetime Democrat, Hatfield a loyal Republican. Both served in the U.S. Navy but came to very different positions on the role of the military in American life. Generally, Hatfield wanted to reduce what he considered excessive military funding, and Carter supported expanding those funds. At first they seemed in agreement on Carter's call for more emphasis on global human rights, but Hatfield gradually backed away from Carter's view when he thought the president was driven more by nationalistic than humanitarian concerns. Hatfield stood strongly against Carter's proposed neutron bomb and also disagreed on SALT II, a proposed treaty with the Soviet Union concerning strategic arms limitations. Hatfield was convinced that Carter's energetic push for additional funding for the military kept funds away from social programs the Oregon senator favored.

Even though these differences existed between Hatfield and Carter, the disagreements did not break their friendship. Hatfield never attacked Carter personally, and well after he left the White House Carter strongly saluted Hatfield. The Oregon senator, Carter stated, was "a genuinely devout believer in Christ who sought to put Christ's teachings into practice."

Binds and breaks also typified the Hatfield-Reagan relationship. First, the similarities: both had served as western governors; Hatfield was a lifetime Oregonian and Reagan had resided in California for nearly forty-five years when he entered the White House in 1981; both were Republicans, although at nearly opposite ends of the party.

The differences were more numerous and often very clear. Reagan had made a name for himself as a speaker for Barry Goldwater in the election of 1964 and later as California governor (1967–75). When Reagan began his run for the presidency in 1976, Hatfield instead supported incumbent Gerald Ford. Reagan followed a platform more akin to the Robert Taft–Barry Goldwater than the Nelson Rockefeller–Mark Hatfield form of Republicanism.

The major Hatfield-Reagan conflicts came concerning military and social welfare spending. When Hatfield was chairman of the Senate Appropriations Committee, from 1981 to 1987, the conflicts over funding became headline news. As the new Appropriations chair, Hatfield continued his familiar patterns in spending: do not allow military funding to get out of control, especially if it steals away from needed dollars for social programs. Reagan's philosophy was just opposite; like many conservative Republicans, he was convinced that a strong—or even stronger—military would not only protect the United States but discourage the Russians from continuing the cold war with escalating military costs.

In his final book, *Against the Grain,* in looking back on his dealings with the president Hatfield admitted that his "relationship with Reagan wasn't always friendly." In fact, Hatfield allowed even further that "the president had reason to be testy with me." Consider the words Hatfield used in reacting to some of Reagan's policies: the president's unusual Star Wars dream was "a terrifying proposal"; his Pentagon program a "technical nightmare, riddled with inefficiencies"; his expansive defense budget "neither sound nor fiscally responsible"; and his deficit spending "a floating crap game." Hatfield's vocabulary overflowed with negative words in reference to Reagan's programs.

In addition to the important legislation and budget matters coming out of his work as chair of the Appropriations Committee, Hatfield was also introducing other bills as a senator. Several dealt with important Oregon matters. As he had throughout his political career, Hatfield pushed for legislation to help Indian tribes. Some of these measures dealt with the Umpqua, Paiute, and Siletz groups, including additional recognition, needed financial support, and reservation expansion. Other legislation Hatfield introduced focused on land exchanges and water compacts, included new areas under the Wild and Scenic Rivers Act, brought in new lands under national forests, and corrected or expanded boundaries of national parks. These bills were other clear examples of Hatfield's focus on measures that would aid in the expansion and protection of Oregon interests.

As reelection time came into view in 1984, Democrats faced their familiar challenge: who could they get to give a good run against Hatfield? No seasoned, well-known political leader came forward, but energetic, ambitious newcomer Margie Hendriksen did. Only four years in the Oregon legislature, she was able to win the Democratic primary in the spring and geared up to go after Hatfield.

An unexpected bomb exploded in July, giving Hendriksen dramatic new possibilities. Investigative columnist Jack Anderson blasted Hatfield in a *Washington Post* expose suggesting that he and his wife had taken slush funds from a crooked Greek entrepreneur, Basil Tsakos, to help push the latter's proposed oil pipeline across Africa. In a telephone interview from Portland, Hatfield refuted the charges to another *Post* journalist. He and Antoinette, Hatfield said, had always "maintained very separate and distinct professorial careers." The money she had received from the Tsakos family was to help the Greek couple land an upscale apartment in Washington, D.C. True enough, Hatfield added, he had publicly supported the trans-Africa pipeline—but because it was a good idea, not because the Tsakos family had given Antoinette $55,000 in total real estate payments.

Hatfield claimed no bribery was involved, but it was an election year and the senator's opponents were always looking for the hard-to-find issues to undercut Hatfield. So, Hatfield's opponents began to all but accuse him of skullduggery of the worst kind; he was not Saint Mark but a devilish conniver. The personal attacks did not work, although privately Hatfield admitted that they had especially depressed Antoinette. Politically, Hatfield quickly and dramatically drove by his competitor. He zipped past the neophyte Hendriksen 808,152 (66.6 percent) to 406,112 (33.4 percent). It was Hatfield's largest margin of victory in five senatorial races.

Still, the funding controversy galloped on. Sensing the negative reactions to what they considered aboveboard actions, the Hatfields decided nonetheless to give away the $55,000 Antoinette had received from Tsakos, contributing it to the Oregon Health and Science University in Portland. Hatfield requested that the Senate Ethics Committee look into the affair. The Justice Department did the same. Both organizations concluded that no evidence existed that the Hatfields accepted the Tsakos payments as bribes; he was exonerated. Much later evidence did turn up that the Greek businessman would accept a court decision that he attempted bribes—if he did, that meant he would be given a lesser penalty. If one accepts Hatfield's explanations of innocence, and the strongest evidence points that way, Hatfield was not guilty of accepting a bribe. But he made a mistake—perhaps two mistakes: he should have realized that others might think of the payments as bribes, and Antoinette and he should have avoided taking the money; and he should have learned from this mistake sufficiently to avoid another similar miscue that surfaced about seven years later.

The year 1985 opened with both Hatfield's electoral success and the lingering attacks on his character. He chose to move on and not allow the attacks to stymie him. In the first three years of his fourth senatorial term, Hatfield continued, for the most part, his resistance to several of President Reagan's policies. Ongoing was his opposition to expanding military expenditures. It was not that he vetoed all monies to be sent for military defense; in fact, without exception, he continued to support funding for troops and military salaries. It is when a new idea or large expenditure was proposed that Hatfield stood up firm like a fiscal-saving bulldog.

In addition to clamping a lid on Reagan's ongoing requests for increased military expenditures, Hatfield voted against specific military programs of the president. A major opposition Hatfield helped launch was against Reagan's Strategic Defense Initiative (SDI). Popularly known as Star Wars, Reagan's mammoth, idealistic program was intended to deescalate if not end the cold war. It aimed at avoiding a horrendous international nuclear war, especially a do-or-die battle between the United States and the Soviet Union. Reagan hoped that the brilliant scientists who had brought about the dangerous nuclear weapons could now turn their efforts toward bringing about defensive weapons to block or destroy those earlier nuclear weapons.

Hatfield and Edward Kennedy had proposed a plan to deal with these problems in their concise book *Freeze! How You Can Prevent Nuclear War* (1982). Hatfield continued his criticism of Reagan's Star War plans, not because he did not favor ending the threat of nuclear warfare but because he considered Reagan's measure pie-in-the-sky, the wrong kind in all ways.

Hatfield battled Reagan on several other political fields. In the Pacific Northwest, Hatfield criticized Reagan's plan to establish a nuclear dump at Hanford, Washington. He also denounced the president's endeavor to turn over the

Hatfield and Senator Edward Kennedy. Hatfield and Kennedy found common ground on a few controversial issues. In 1982 they coauthored *Freeze*, a book supporting antinuclear efforts. Photo courtesy of the *Oregonian*.

Bonneville Power Administration to private companies. Clashes over timber and water policies continued apace. Nationally, Hatfield and Reagan were far apart on support for domestic social programs dealing with education, health, and food. Throughout Reagan's presidency, Hatfield attempted to rein in military spending so as to aid social programs; his preference was always for the "butter" expenditures in the familiar conflict between guns and butter. On one occasion, Hatfield condemned Reagan's inadequate support for national social needs as "starving, choking, and evisceration." He pointed to a poll ranking the United States forty-ninth in world literacy as an example of Reagan's imbalance for military and against social needs.

The sly Hatfield was not above using guile to get White House approval for his desired legislation. On one occasion when Hatfield was attempting to get the Columbia Gorge named a national park, Reagan contacted the Oregon senator and told him he was planning to veto the national park legislation. Hatfield listened, told the president he understood, and, rather offhandedly, mentioned that several of Reagan's desired requests were "backed up" before the Appropriation Committee and might not get its stamp of approval. Not many days hence, Reagan signed the Columbia River Gorge Scenic Act, one of the few legislative acts concerning environmental issues during his eight years in the White House.

Hatfield did support some of Reagan's policies. For instance, he backed Clarence Thomas for the Supreme Court—and the unsuccessful candidate Robert Bork as well. He also pushed for, generally, the president's goal of reducing cold war competitions and tensions. But he could not stand for Reagan's Star Wars dream, which the Oregon senator considered too idealistic and wrongheaded.

To Hatfield's credit—and to the Reagans'—differences of opinions did not end a friendship. In one memorable evening, President Reagan and his wife Nancy were invited to the Hatfields for one of Antoinette's highly regarded home-cooked meals. Unfortunately, the lights went out in that area of Washington, and Antoinette had to cook via natural gas and in candle light. It was a long-remembered small gathering. This was a pattern that many who knew Hatfield commented on: even though he often differed with presidents and colleagues, those disagreements did not end collegiality.

Hatfield's contacts with President George H. W. Bush gained much less attention than his associations with Reagan. The lesser publicity is all the more interesting since Hatfield and Bush, moderate to progressive Republicans, were closer ideologically than Hatfield and Reagan. Hatfield and Bush had begun their congressional careers together, Hatfield in the Senate and Bush in the House. They had become friends, but Bush left Congress, and he and Hatfield seemed separate until Bush became Reagan's vice president in 1981. Almost nothing is said about Hatfield-Bush meetings during the Reagan presidency.

Probably the most publicized happening bringing Hatfield and Bush together—or separating them further—was Hatfield's vote against Bush's Operation Desert Storm to send American troops to chase Iraqi dictator Saddam Hussein out of Kuwait. Hatfield and Senator Charles Grassley of Iowa were the only two Republicans to vote against their president. Speaking directly about his negative vote, Hatfield stated, "I couldn't believe the American people approved the war in the Gulf. To me, it was nothing but an oil war." The war lasted but a few days in February 1991, and the next month a Gallup poll gave Bush an approval rating of 89 percent, suggesting how far away Hatfield was from public opinion in opposing the war.

Writer James A. Fitzhenry, who served on both the Hatfield and Bush staffs, provided an illuminating comparison of the two political leaders. He saw them as admirable men driven by convictions that "relationships matter," that one must "respect the institutions of government" and a "focus on being good, not great." Fitzhenry also thought both men were unwilling to compromise their values and that their lives reflected the "loyalty and courage" so "rare" among politicians. These positive characteristics, the writer suggested, were why Hatfield and Bush could differ on ideas and actions but never ended a friendship because of differences.

When the Republicans lost the Senate majority in the election of 1986, that meant Hatfield's chairmanship of the Appropriations Committee ended the next year. Rather than deal with the president's call for larger defense and military budgets, Hatfield turned increasingly to pushing for measures particularly helpful for Oregonians, so much so that he was accused of filling up the "pork barrel" for his home state. He continued to support Oregon Health and Science University, which was launched when he was governor; backed the Portland MAX or Light Rail system, begun when he was chairing the Appropriations Committee; and tried to get the federal government to pay more attention to the needs of logging communities, agriculturists, and the sick and needy.

Hatfield also continued his hectic speaking and writing schedule. Increasingly, he was asked to speak at prayer breakfasts, college graduations, and evangelical gatherings of a wide assortment. Although Hatfield did not author a new book in the 1980s save for the coauthored *Freeze!*, he wrote dozens of essays, book forewords, and introductions. More and more he was seen as a spokesman-leader among academic and more progressive evangelicals.

Hatfield was not prepared for the close run for reelection that emerged suddenly in 1990. His opponent Harry Lonsdale, a Ph.D. researcher and well-to-do businessman, fired two broadsides at Hatfield: at his antiabortion stance, and at his too-close ties to loggers and his willingness to cut old growth timber. As the campaign wore on toward fall, Lonsdale pulled even and slightly ahead of Hatfield. Realizing he was in a horse race, the incumbent abandoned his aloof, sedate campaigning and went after Lonsdale in an avalanche of radio, television, and newspaper advertisements. He accused Lonsdale's company of dumping poisonous wastes into water sources. The Hatfield campaign charges proved effective. Hatfield garnered 590,095 votes (53.8 percent) to Lonsdale's 507,743 (46.2 percent). Although the final tally was not close, it was Hatfield's closest run for the Senate after his first with Robert Duncan.

The euphoria of winning another taxing election quickly disappeared. A deluge of newspapers stories attacking Hatfield's actions in the Senate began to appear in 1991 and stretched on into 1992. Most were explicit or veiled attacks on him and his actions as person and politician. Hatfield was crestfallen from the criticisms in the first years of his fifth and final term in the Senate.

The charges against Hatfield were numerous and varied. The most repeated accusation was that James Holderman, former president of the University of South Carolina, had used gifts of art, plane tickets, and a scholarship for the Hatfields' son Visko to gain Hatfield's support for a new engineering building at the university. Other charges included special treatment of daughter Elizabeth at the Oregon Health and Science University in "payment" for huge grants the federal government had given the university through the Senate Appropriation Committee. In addition, critics pointed to a loan from John Dellenbach, Hatfield's good friend and former U.S. congressman from Medford, who loaned the senator money and later encouraged him to support funding for a Christian college organization for which he worked.

The Justice Department, but even more assiduously the Senate Ethics Committee, examined the charges and issued Hatfield a "stern rebuke." The Ethics Committee concluded that Hatfield had not "intentionally failed" to report the gifts but nonetheless had engaged in "inappropriate" acts that violated Senate guidelines.

Not surprisingly, more than a few Hatfield opponents and those who viewed the moniker "St. Mark" cynically were ready to conclude that Hatfield had indeed "sullied" his supposed shining image by his illegal actions. The *New York Times, Washington Post,* and Portland *Oregonian* reported on the disappointing story, but the *Seattle Times* seemed to joy in commenting on the now-"sullied" reputation of the "Once-Invincible" politician.

Hatfield, according to acquaintances, was "saddened and somewhat chastened by the controversy." He thought the accusations might blot out what could "be the final chapter of a 40-year career in public service." Still, the senator was apologetic about what had happened. "My mistakes were many," he stated, "and my omissions were serious. There is no one but myself to blame." When Hatfield prepared his final book, a memoir, in 2000, he made no specific mention of the Tsakos or Holderman incidents. They were mistakes he clearly wished to forget.

Hatfield first began serving in his fifth senatorial term with Bill Clinton as president when the former young Arkansas governor upset incumbent George H. W. Bush in the election of 1992 and moved into the White House. Even though Clinton was a Democrat, Hatfield got along better with him than with fellow Republican Ronald Reagan and perhaps as well as with George H. W. Bush. Hatfield agreed, for the most part, with Clinton's disciplined fiscal policies and certainly supported that president's welfare and deregulation programs. Generally, Hatfield's economic goals were similar to those of Clinton; most important, balance the budget, rein in military spending, and find monies for social needs. He did vote against Clinton's sending troops to Bosnia, however. The Oregon senator said very little about Clinton's moral failures and the subsequent impeachment trial. The conflicts with Clinton were minimal. And in the Senate's retirement celebration for Hatfield in July 1996, Clinton saluted Hatfield's consistency, his opposition to nuclear weapons and war; he was, the president added, a person "who has lived his convictions as well as any person I have ever known in public life." Clinton summed up his view in one memorable sentence: because Hatfield "has tried to love his enemies, he has no enemies."

When the Republicans again gained the Senate majority in the election of 1994, Hatfield reassumed the chairmanship of the Appropriations Committee. Meanwhile, under the ramrod leadership of Congressman Newt Gingrich, the Republicans were launching their "Contract with America" program. The program included a possible constitutional amendment that would control congressional spending through a balanced budget. In reactions to this balanced budget controversy, Hatfield once again epitomized his "Stand Alone or Go Home" position that his colleagues had come to know.

Hatfield let it be known, early on, that he would not support the proposed constitutional amendment. The proposal was misleading, Hatfield began; it showed Congress was unwilling, on its own, to place a lid on spending, particularly on military expenditures. Besides, a constitutional amendment with spending limits would likely reduce the much-needed funding for social programs for health, education, and welfare, all of which the Oregon senator supported. Moreover, including the provision in the amendment that spending limits could be bypassed if two-thirds of the Congress voted such only prepared the way for many such bypasses, as Congress had proven in the recent past. For Hatfield, the proposed amendment was a flawed idea, not worthy of support.

As the vote on the amendment neared, it became clear that Republican senatorial leaders such as Bob Dole and Orrin Hatch needed every party member's vote, but they did not have Hatfield's. They tried to cajole him into voting for the amendment. When the pressure mounted just before the floor vote, Hatfield even offered to resign so that his missing vote could allow the measure to pass. No, Dole responded, that would not do. The amendment failed. Some young conservative Republicans were so upset that they pushed to have Hatfield removed from the Appropriations leadership. Junior Oregon senator Robert Packwood, however, denounced that move as "political cannibalism."

Although controversies over Hatfield's gift receiving and his vote against the balanced budget captured most attention in the Oregon senator's final term, his introduction and push for several measures were testaments of his ongoing emphases. Nothing captured more of Hatfield's support than bills to expand funding for health and medical treatment and research. He focused particularly on the health needs of seniors, especially those inflicted with Alzheimer's disease. He also pushed for limits to be placed on military spending and introduced several bills to outlaw landmines. No less emphasized was funding for educational needs, including more support for teachers and additional funding for libraries. Students of American history were pleased, too, to see Hatfield introducing legislation to fund the National Historical Publications and Records Commission.

Hatfield likewise delivered on what he considered Oregon's major needs. He introduced several bills to help the struggling lumber industry as well as measures to protect land and water resources. His support for Indian tribes also appeared in several bills. The Oregon Trail, Bonneville Power Administration, Columbia River water conservation, and medical and health facilities in Oregon likewise benefited from Hatfield's support.

The upset over the balanced budget was added evidence, Hatfield thought, that it was time for him to retire. Soon after that dogfight, on 1 December 1995, in Silverton, Oregon, Hatfield announced that he would soon finish his long senatorial career and not run for reelection. That decision was now certain.

On 3 January 1997, Hatfield completed his almost thirty years in the Senate and quickly returned to Oregon. While still in the Senate and looking to retirement, he let it be known that he would like to return to the classroom. His seven years teaching political science at Willamette University were fond memories. He wanted to become a professor again.

In his year of retirement from the Senate, Hatfield began teaching at George Fox University. He offered courses, off and on, for nearly ten years (1997–2007). His teaching colleagues—among them Lee Nash, Ralph Beebe, Mark David Hall, Lon Fendall—fondly remembered team-teaching

Hatfield and Lee Nash at George Fox University. After retirement from the U.S. Senate in 1997, Hatfield returned to the classroom. At George Fox University, he team-taught classes with much-admired professor and administrator Lee Nash. Hatfield 2, Photograph, GFU.01.09, George Fox Photographs, George Fox University Archives, Newberg, Oregon.

assignments with Hatfield. Over the years he offered such courses as The Vietnam Experience, Herbert Hoover and His Times, Christianity and Politics in the U.S., Campaigns and Elections, and Presidential/Congressional Relationship. Students in Hatfield's classes were getting on-the-spot experiences from their noted politician/professor as well as strong academic offerings. Not satisfied to inhabit just one campus, Hatfield also gave courses at Willamette University and Portland State University.

Besides his teaching stints, Hatfield prepared his final book, *Against the Grain,* and continued to give sporadic speeches and presentations. He especially joyed in visiting the Oregon coast, where he and Antoinette had purchased a home.

Then Hatfield's health began to fail. Adding to the decline was a bad fall. In November 2010, Hatfield entered a hospital for observation in the Washington, D.C. area, a hospital carrying his name.

Death came at age eighty-nine on 7 August 2011 in a special care unit in Portland, and burial followed at Willamette National Cemetery in Portland. The cause of death was not revealed. Shortly afterwards, a flood of salutary stories about Hatfield and his important political journey filled numerous newspapers and magazines.

Epilogue

Mark Hatfield piled up memorable statistics in his almost half century as a political leader. Historians, biographers, and journalists, among others, have listed several notable accomplishments in Hatfield's changing roles as state legislator and secretary of state, governor, and U.S. senator.

Most emphasized is that Hatfield never lost an election from his first to his final campaign, from 1950 to 1990. Overall, Hatfield won eleven elections, three to the Oregon legislature—one as secretary of state, two as governor, and five as U.S. senator. Two or three of these elections were fairly close, but most were decisive victories. These victories were even more impressive when one considers that during these forty years of elections Hatfield as a Republican was always in the minority party in Oregon. He had to win over Democrats to be continually victorious.

Most commentators on Hatfield's career, even Hatfield himself, have had difficulty in finding a term that satisfactorily defines his political position. Hatfield spoke of himself as a "liberal," "progressive," "radical," or sometimes a "moderate" Republican. But he did not consistently use the same term. Hatfield interpreters have encountered the same problem.

Democrats, by and large, thought of Governor Hatfield as too focused on business interests, so tied to entrepreneurial issues that he overlooked welfare needs. Opponents also thought he spent too much time out of state, grooming himself for national office. Foes also were convinced that Hatfield wanted to revise the state's constitution and its government structure so as to give himself more power as governor. It was a "power grab," they said.

Some Republicans had opposite complaints. Hard-core conservatives thought Hatfield spent too much money, especially on welfare plans they would not support. The traditionalists also wanted the governor to keep tax rates down, in some cases even lower them. Nor did the conservatives want a revised state constitution or a reorganized executive branch. They wanted to leave things as they were. More than a few fellow Republicans also thought Hatfield catered far too much and too often to labor groups. For these dissenters, workers belonged with the Democrats, where they had usually been since the 1930s.

Few observers of Hatfield's eight years as governor clearly understood his political stances. He was not an "either-or" but a "both-and" leader. Putting things differently, viewing Oregon politics across a broad spectrum from left-leaning Democrats to right-moving Republicans, Hatfield was most often a middle-of-the-road politician, favoring some elements of an issue, disagreeing with others. Consider his stances on business-labor issues. He repeatedly encouraged small businesses in Oregon, looking for ways to support them in times of challenge. Yet he also often worked diligently with labor leaders to hear and help settle workers' complaints. Think also of Hatfield's never-ending work with welfare issues. He pushed for programs for the sick and poor, for students, for teachers. But just as often he labored to keep spending on these needs within the state budgets. Reflect in addition on Hatfield's dealings with state-federal challenges. Most often, Hatfield, like most loyal Republicans of his time, wanted to keep power at the local level—within the state and down to communities. Still, when President

Lyndon Johnson offered several programs within his War on Poverty, Hatfield made sure that Oregon benefited from these "pork barrel" handouts. In another, even more controversial area, Hatfield displayed his complex leadership. Enthusiastic environmentalists often criticized Hatfield for being too cozy with lumber interests. They often dunned him for allowing too much cutting of old growth timber. Hatfield maintained still another middle-of-the-road stance on these issues. Yes, he would allow some cutting of old growth timber because to lock up all those logs was to abandon those who needed work and income and a state needing revenue. The governor would try to do both: to cut and conserve carefully but also to support workers and their families and the state. Seeing Mark Hatfield as a complex, two-way politician, not as an either-or politician, provides a more comprehensive, revealing explanation of his political views and actions.

Hatfield's dualistic approach to politics as governor owed much to Herbert Hoover, who, along with Abraham Lincoln, was a Hatfield hero. Hatfield was drawn to several parts of Hoover's credo. In his master's thesis on Hoover at Stanford, in his work on the Hoover Commission or Report, and in his reading of Hoover's book *Challenge of Liberty* (1934), Hatfield was introduced to and won over to several of Hoover's ideas. These included two-way points of view: a strong executive but not a huge, overweening central government such as arose in the New Deal; centralizing power for direct, efficient action but not at the expense of citizens, communities, and states; policies that helped the body public *and* individual Americans. Hatfield was also much drawn to Hoover's gigantic delivery of foodstuffs to a decimated Europe at the end of World War I and tried to build on that efficient and energetic plan as a senator pushing for food help around the globe.

One should also keep in mind that Hatfield rose to political eminence alongside several other notable political figures from the Pacific Northwest. These leaders became well known as regional or national lawmakers. They included Senator Frank Church, Governor Robert Smylie, and governor and cabinet member Cecil B. Andrus of Idaho; Senator Henry "Scoop" Jackson and Governor Dan Evans of Washington; and Governor Tom McCall of Oregon. Together, these state and national politicians brought country-wide attention to their leadership and caused the nation to reconsider its attitudes about political activities in the Pacific Northwest from the 1950s to the 1980s. Mark Hatfield was very much at the center of this notable coterie of Northwest political statesmen.

Another part of Hatfield's story as Oregon governor deserves summing up. He rose to political office as a Republican but served in a state experiencing a Democratic surge. From 1951 to 1967, as Hatfield was in office as a state legislator, secretary of state, and then governor, he faced a Democratic Party increasingly expanding in numbers. That being the case, one has to ask: how did Mark Hatfield rise so quickly and continuously in Oregon politics and become a nationally known figure when he came from the minority party in his state?

This difficult question is not easily answered. Yet a few specifics help explain Hatfield's unparalleled popularity and successes in Oregon politics. First of all, his physical appearance impressed nearly everyone; he was young, handsome, well dressed, and exuded energy. Second, he seemed omnipresent, weekly—almost daily—making speeches, meeting with lay and government groups, taking part in political and community gatherings. Third, he was a cheerleader for Oregon. Early on convinced that economic needs should be the top priority for Oregon political leaders, he committed himself to bring new businesses, industries, and tourists to the state; and these newcomers would, in turn, create new jobs. Fourth, he was a lifelong independent person. Although a Republican, an evangelical, and an ambitious politician, he moved primarily in his own directions, challenging party leaders and religious and cultural traditions. Finally, Hatfield exuded personal dependability. As a son, husband, father, and leader, Hatfield spoke and acted in confidence-enhancing ways. One could depend on Mark Hatfield; his footprints followed his spoken and written words. Even if one traveled up paths different from those of Hatfield—as a Democrat, a nonbeliever, a woman, or a minority—one could trust him. That trustworthiness was a key ingredient in the unparalleled successes of his forty-six-year political career.

Hatfield was not a flawless, always-right saint, of course, as his opponents often tried to make clear. On occasion he moved too quickly, based on his personal preferences and not on public opinion or established facts. His continued push for executive reorganization and revision of the Oregon constitution failed to attract clear majority support. His net receipts or broaden-the-base tax idea, although often urged upon the legislature, never got on track with the state's lawmakers. His strong push for a graduate research center in Portland, a good and acceptable idea, failed in large part because the governor could not rally Oregon higher education leaders or find the necessary financial support. And the Hatfield mistakes revealed in the 1980s and 1990s confirmed his humanity.

So, on balance, what is one to conclude about Mark Hatfield as governor and as state and national politician? We see that he made mistakes and sometimes pushed ahead of voters with his strong personal views. Still, consider the numerous contributions Hatfield made to state and national politics. They include strong and energetic leadership; boosting Oregon's economy; contributions to education; committed servanthood as a politician; an inspiring example of how personal faith and politics could integrate and work smoothly. He was a balanced leader. Well-known western writer Wallace Stegner once wrote, "I have been convinced for a long time . . . that what is mistakenly called the middle of the road is actually the most radical and difficult position—much more difficult and radical than either reaction or rebellion." Stegner could well have been speaking of Mark Hatfield.

The strengths mounted up and stand, placing Hatfield at the pinnacle of Oregon and western politicians who clearly influenced local, state, regional, and national politics.

Essay on Sources

This study is based on a thorough examination of the published, and selected unpublished, sources available on Mark O. Hatfield. Full citations for the books and essays, some of the newspaper articles, and other sources appear in the accompanying bibliography. Here only the most pertinent sources receive comment; the bibliography lists many more helpful items.

Full-length book coverage of the life and career of Mark Hatfield is minimal. The paucity of such extensive accounts is largely because the most extensive collection of Hatfield materials remains closed at the Willamette University Mark Hatfield Library. Other sources are available, but the most comprehensive Hatfield manuscript collection will not open until July 2022.

As a result, this brief political biography is based on other sources. First, the books by Mark Hatfield. His first book, *Not Quite to Simple* (1968), is a well-written account, particularly on Hatfield's early life, his first years as an Oregon politician, his eight years as governor, and his opposition to the Vietnam War. Hatfield's final book, *Against the Grain: Reflections of a Rebel Republican* (with Diane N. Solomon,

2001), is an informal memoir studded with valuable reflections. *Between the Rock and the Hard Place* (1976), partially drafted by Hatfield assistant Wesley Granberg-Michaelson, is particularly valuable for seeing the overlapping of Hatfield's religious faith and political activities. Hatfield's *Conflict and Conscience* (1971) deals with the same topics but focuses more on faith than politics. *Freeze! How You Can Help Prevent Nuclear War* (1982), coauthored with Edward Kennedy, treats an important topic of Hatfield's focus after the Vietnam War. Over time, Hatfield contributed numerous introductions, prefaces, and essays to a wide spectrum of books but particularly with an evangelical focus.

The sole limited, now dated, biography of Hatfield is Robert Eells and Bartell Nyberg, *Lonely Walk: The Life of Senator Mark Hatfield* (1979). A revision of Eells's doctoral dissertation (1976), this brief life story emphasizes Hatfield's commitment to what the authors call his "radical Anabaptist" belief system. One wishes the authors had included fewer long, block quotes and more political narrative and evaluation. Still, the book remains the best extant biographical study of Hatfield.

Other writers have zeroed in on Hatfield's evangelical faith and shown how that powerful set of beliefs shaped his politics. Particularly helpful in this regard is Lon Fendall's smoothly written *Stand Alone or Come Home: Mark Hatfield as an Evangelical and a Progressive* (2008). Wesley Granberg-Michaelson's autobiographical volume, *Unexpected Destinations: An Evangelical Pilgrimage to World Christianity* (2011), illuminates his own search for balance between religious commitment and life journey and does the same for Hatfield in his early senatorial years.

The present account also relies heavily on newspaper sources. It draws on essays in the *New York Times,* the *Washington Post,* and several Oregon newspapers. More than any other newspaper, the Portland *Oregonian* has been a much-relied-upon source.

For general Oregon history, particularly its political history, this biography utilizes a clutch of strong historical overviews. On Oregon, two books have been particularly helpful: William G. Robbins, *This Storied Land* (2005, 2020), and David Peterson del Mar, *Oregon's Promise: An Interpretive History* (2003). Especially of aid in examining political trends in Oregon and the American West is Walter Nugent, *Color Coded: Party Politics in the American West 1950–2016* (2018).

Following "fair use" guidelines, I quote Hatfield words only from his and other published works and those in newspapers. The quotes are kept to a minimum. No unpublished writings by Hatfield are quoted in this work.

Bibliography

This extensive listing of writings by and about Mark Hatfield is primarily limited to print sources, although major manuscript holdings containing Hatfield materials are also listed. Those wishing additional sources, including recorded or audio books, photographs and graphics, computer-filed research, Oregon state and national government documents, and additional manuscript collections, should check with World Cat, the huge bibliographical listing containing a near-exhaustive catalogue of materials by and about Hatfield.

BOOKS BY HATFIELD

Against the Grain: Reflections of a Rebel Republican. Ashland, OR: White Cloud Press, 2001 (with Diane N. Solomon).

Amnesty? The Unsettled Question of Vietnam. Lawrence, MA: Sun River Press, 1973 (with Arlie Schardt and William A. Rusher).

Between a Rock and a Hard Place. Waco, TX: Word Books, 1976.

Conflict and Conscience. Waco, TX: Word Books, 1971.

Freeze! How You Can Help Prevent Nuclear War. New York: Bantam, 1982 (with Edward Kennedy).

"Herbert Hoover and Labor: Policies and Attitudes, 1897–1928." MA thesis, Stanford University, 1948.

Herbert Hoover and His Times: A Course of Study and Its Researches. Newberg, OR: George Fox University, 2004 (editor, with Lee Nash).

Bibliography

Herbert Hoover Reassessed: Essays. Washington, DC: USGPO, 1981 (editor).

Not Quite So Simple. New York: Harper & Row, 1968.

Vice Presidents of the United States: 1789–1993. Washington, DC: U.S. Government Printing Office, 1997 (editor, with Wendy Wolff).

ESSAYS BY HATFIELD

"Abortion: A Legislator Speaks." *Reformed Journal* 23 (September 1973): 11–14.

"The Absence of Political Will in the United States." In William J. Byron, ed., *Causes of World Hunger.* New York: Paulist Press, 1982.

"Address to the Harvard Young Republican Club." In *Vietnam: A Resource Collection of Statements, Clippings and Other Documents.* Akron, PA: Mennonite Central Committee, 1967.

"After Containment: A New Foreign Policy for the 1990s." *SAIS Review* 11 (Winter-Spring 1991): 1–10 (with Matthew R. McHugh).

"American Democracy and American Evangelicalism—New Perspectives." *Theology News and Notes* 14 (November 1970): 8–11.

"America's Need for an 'Ethical Renaissance.'" *Journal of Business Ethics* 1 (May 1982): 99–108.

"Between a Rock and a Hard Place." In John MacArthur, et al., *Perfecting the Saints: The Progress of Perfection.* Waco, TX: Focus, 1976.

"Beyond Watergate: Five Ways to Rebuild Confidence." *Washington Post Outlook,* 26 August 1973, 1–2.

Book review of Clifford R. Miller, *Baptists and the Oregon Frontier.* In *Oregon Historical Quarterly* 69 (December 1968): 324–25.

Book review of George H. Nash, *The Life of Herbert Hoover.* In *Presidential Studies Quarterly* 14 (Winter 1984): 134–35.

Book review of Peter Iverson, *Barry Goldwater, Native Arizonian.* In *Pacific Historical Review* 67 (May 1998): 309–10.

Book review of Woody Klein, *Let in the Sun.* In Portland *Oregonian,* 8 November 1964, 83.

"Bringing Political Power Back Home: The Case for Neighborhood Government." *Ripon Quarterly* 1 (Summer 1974): 19–26.

"A Bulletin from Capitol Hill." *Science and Children* 29 (March 1991): 30–31.

"Can a Christian Be a Politician?" (interview) *His* 28 (October 1967): 1–5.

"The Case for Dedicated Funding." In Claude E. Barfield and Bruce L. R. Smith, eds., *The Future of Biomedical Research.* Washington, DC: AEI Press: Brookings Institution, 1997.

Bibliography

"A Change of Heart." In Phyllis Hube, ed., *The Meaning of Christmas.* Philadelphia: A. J. Holman, 1975.

"Christ and Caesar." In Norvel Hadley, ed., *New Call to Peacemaking: A Challenge to All Friends.* Philadelphia, PA, and Plainfield, IN: Faith and Life Movement, 1976.

"Christian Foundations in American Government." *Review and Expositor* 65 (Summer 1968): 283–86.

"The Christian Is Needed in Public Service." *Baptist Outlook* 10 (Winter 1959).

"Christianity and Politics." *Freedom Now,* Part 1, 4 (September–October 1968): 14–19; Part 2 (November-December 1968): 23–29.

"Christ's Call to Service." In James M. Skillen, ed., *Confessing Christ and Doing Politics.* Washington, DC: Association for Public Justice Education, Fund, 1982, 11–18.

"Church and State—Politics and the Christian Church." In *Veritas Considered: In Celebration of Harvard University's 350th Anniversary.* Cambridge, MA: Harvard-Ratcliffe Christian Fellowship, 1986.

"The Church Must Rescue the American Family." *Lutheran Standard* 16 (16 March 1976).

"Clear the Air." *Environmental Law* 22 (1992): 791–95 (with Brian Blum).

"Committed to an Ideal." *Collegiate Challenge* 1 (October 1961).

"Consensus in the Klamath." *Environmental Law* 26 (Spring 1996): 447–48.

Contributor, to Vernon K. McLellan, ed., *Billy Graham: A Tribute from Friends.* New York: Warner Books, 2002.

Contributor, to Wesley G. Pippert, *Faith at the Top.* Elgin, IL: Cook, 1973.

Contributor, to William D. Apel, *Witness before Dawn: Exploring the Meaning of Christian Life.* Valley Forge, PA: Judson Press, 1984.

"Crisis in American Leadership." *Eternity* 24 (July 1973): 10–11, 24–25.

"Does the System Work?" *Portland Oregonian Northwest Magazine,* 25 July 1971, 8–10.

"The Draft Law Should Be Abolished." *Saturday Evening Post* 240 (1 July 1967): 12, 14.

"An Economics for Sustaining Humanity." *Post American* 4 (March 1975).

"Energy Crisis." In Waldo W. Braden, ed., *Representative American Speeches, 1973–1974.* New York: H. W. Wilson, 1974.

"The Erosion of the Lordship of Jesus Christ." *Eternity* 15 (August 1964): 10–13.

Bibliography

"The Essence of Fellowship." *Christ for the Nations* 28 (November 1974).

"Evangelicalism and Coming World Peace." In George M. Wilson, ed., *Evangelicalism Now.* Minneapolis, MN: World Wide Publications, 1970.

"Facing the Vietnam Issue 11." *Ripon Forum* 7 (November 1971): 16–17.

"Foreign Policy in a Transition Era." *Alfred M. Landon Lectures on Public Issues* 1. Manhattan: Kansas State University, 1982.

"Foreword," to Charles F. Cooley, *Memoirs of a CO: Obeying the Commandment, Trusting the Beatitude.* Columbus, OH: Charles F. Cooley, 2000.

"Foreword," to Charles R. Swindoll, *Killing Giants, Pulling Thorns.* Portland, OR: Multnomah Press, 1978.

"Foreword," to Clay Cooper, ed., *Nothing to Win but the World: Missions at the Crossroads.* Grand Rapids, MI: Zondervan, 1965.

"Foreword," to Daniel B. Leavitt, *Cogwheeling with History: Eyewitness to an Awesome Age.* Jaffrey, NH: Savron Graphics, 2000.

"Foreword," to Eddy Swieson, *Pause for Prayer: A Collection of Meditative Prayers.* [Washington, DC?]: The Author, 1976.

"Foreword," to George H. Nash, *Herbert Hoover and Stanford University.* Stanford, CA: Hoover Institute Press of Stanford University, 1999.

"Foreword," to Gert Boyle, *One Tough Mother: Taking Charge in Life, Business, and Apple Pies.* New York: Basic Books, 2006.

"Foreword," to Gordon C. Bennett, *The New Abolitionists: The Story of Nuclear Free Zones.* Elgin, IL: Brethren Press, 1987.

"Foreword," to Henri J. M. Nouwen, *With Open Hands.* New York: Ballantine Books, 1972, 1990.

"Foreword," to Jeb Stuart Magruder, *From Power to Peace.* Waco, TX: Word Books, 1978.

"Foreword," to Jerzy Lerski, *Herbert Hoover and Poland: A Documentary History of a Friendship.* Stanford, CA: Hoover Institution Press, 1977.

"Foreword," to John O'Sullivan and Alan M. Meckler, eds., *The Draft and Its Enemies: A Documentary History.* Urbana: University of Illinois Press, 1974.

"Foreword," to John Perkins, *Let Justice Roll Down.* Grand Rapids, MI: Family Christian Press, 1976, 2001.

"Foreword," to John Redekop, *The American Far Right.* Grand Rapids, MI: Eerdmans, 1968.

Bibliography

"Foreword," to John Salisbury, *A Message for Americans*. Portland, OR: Binfords and Mort, 1965.

"Foreword," to Kristine Olson, *Standing Tall: The Lifeway of Kathryn Jones Harrison*. Seattle: University of Washington Press, 2005.

"Foreword," to Lon Fendall, *Citizenship, a Christian Calling*. Newberg, OR: Barclay Press, 2003.

"Foreword," to Robert C. Larson, *Wansui: Insights on China Today*. Waco, TX: Word Books, 1974.

"Foreword," to *Seven Months to Oregon: 1853 Diaries, Letters and Reminiscent Accounts*. Tooele, UT: Patrice Press, 2008.

"Foreword," to Sharon P. Price, *Just Being Sharon*. Monmouth, OR: Drift Creek Press, 1996.

"Foreword," to Thayer C. Willis, *Navigating the Dark Side of Wealth: A Life Guide for Inheritors*. Portland, OR: New Concord Press, 2003

"Foreword," to Vivian Corbett Atterbury, *The Oregon Story*. Portland: Binfords & Mort, 1959.

"Foreword," to William S. Deal, *The Soul-Winner's Guide: A Training Manual for Soul- Winning*. Grand Rapids, MI: Zondervan, 1960.

"Global Interdependence: 'Life, Liberty, and the Pursuit of Happiness' in Today's World." In Waldo W. Braden, ed., *Representative American Speeches, 1974-1975*. New York: H. W. Wilson, 1975.

"God's Call to America." *Church Herald* 42 (28 December 1973).

"Gov. Hatfield Outlines Post-Goldwater Views." Portland *Oregonian*, 18 December 1964, 42.

"The Gray Areas of Faith and Politics." *His* 39 (November 1978): 16–18, 22.

"The Greed of Man and the Will of God." *The Other Side* 10 (November-December 1974): 8–13, 62–64.

"Hands and Feet to Faith." In Douglas L. Koopman and Paul B. Henry, *Serving the Claims of Justice: The Thoughts of Paul B. Henry*. Grand Rapids, MI: Calvin College Alumni Association, 2001.

"Hatfield Takes Note of Achievements, Challenges to Come." Portland *Oregonian*, 31 December 1961.

"Herbert Hoover and the Conservation of Human and Natural Resources." In Lee M. Nash, ed., *Understanding Hoover: Ten Perspectives*. Stanford, CA: Hoover Institution Press, 1987.

"Herbert Hoover as an Enduring Model for American Leaders." In Paul N. Anderson and Howard R. Macy, eds., *Truth's Bright Embrace: Essays and Poems in Honor of Arthur Roberts*. Newberg, OR: George Fox University Press, 1996.

Bibliography

"Honest Arms Control and Political Realism." In Dale W. Brown, ed., *What About the Russians? A Christian Approach to US-Soviet Conflict*. Elgin, IL: Brethren Press, 1984.

"How Can a Christian Be in Politics?" In Robert Clouse et al., eds., *Protest and Politics*. Greenwood, SC: Attic Press, 1968, 7–22.

"How I Became a Christian." *His* 20 (May 1960): 5–6.

"How to Get Involved." *Christian Life* 38 (July 1976).

"If We Fall Down in the Land of Peace." In Waldo W. Braden, ed., *Representative American Speeches, 1979–1980*. New York: H. W. Wilson, 1980.

"The Illusion of Arms Control." *Sojourners* 8 (February 1979): 6–9.

"Indispensable Man." *Journal of Democracy* 6 (1995): 165–69.

"In Whom Do We Really Trust?" *Eternity* 22 (May 1971): 10.

"Introduction," to E. Raymond Wilson, *Uphill for Peace*. Richmond, IN: Friends United Press, 1975.

"Introduction," to *The Economics of Defense: A Bipartisan Review of Military Spending*. New York: Praeger, 1971.

"Introduction," to Gene Sharp, *Social Power and Political Freedom*. Boston: Albert Einstein Institution, 1978.

"Introduction," to John Allen Lapp, *A Dream for America*. New York: Pillar Books, 1976.

"Introduction," to John Foxe and Hilda Hoel Schroetter, *Foxe's Book of English Martyrs: Reformation Heroes Who Paid the Price for Our Religious and Political Freedom*. Waco, TX: Word Books, 1981.

"Introduction," to Joseph D. Ben-Dak and Ramzi H. Malik, *Children of Abraham: Toward a New Spirit in the Near East*. Washington, DC: Institutional Development and Economic Affairs Service, 1974.

"Introduction," to Paul B. Henry, *Politics for Evangelicals*. Valley Forge, PA: Judson Press, 1974.

"Introduction," to Vernon Grounds, *Revolution and the Christian Faith: An Evangelical Perspective*. Eugene, OR: Wipf and Stock, [1971] 2007.

"Introduction," to William Wilberforce, *Real Christianity: Discerning True and False Faith*. In James M. Houston, ed. Minneapolis, MN: Bethany House Publishers, [1982] 1997.

"Is the Proposed Pursuit of U.S. 'Energy Independence' a Sound National Policy?" *Congressional Digest* 54 (August–September 1975).

"Laity and Clergy as People of God." *Theology Today* 36 (1 January 1980): 553–55.

"Lenten Guideposts." *Guideposts* (February 1960); reprinted in *Portland Oregonian*, 7 February 1960; 1 April 1961.

Bibliography

"Living with Purpose." *Campus Ambassador* (January–February 1965).

"The Long's Peak Working Group and River Basin Trusts." *Environmental Law* 24 (1994): 145–56.

"Making the Right Choice." *Compact* (October 1969).

"Mentor to a Senator." In J. Brent Walker, ed., *James Dunn: Champion for Religious Liberty.* Macon, GA: Smyth & Helwys, 1999.

"Minimum Deposits for Beverage Containers: National Impact and Current Federal Legislation." *Boston College Environmental Affairs Law Review* 8 (December 1979) (with Stephen J. Owens).

"Missionaries and the CIA." *Christian Herald* 99 (March 1976): 13, 32.

"Moral Majority or Servant Minority." In James B. Stockdale, ed., *The Ethics of Citizenship.* Dallas: University of Texas at Dallas, 1980, 1981.

"The Nation Needs a Bioethics Commission." *Science and Technology* 11 (Winter 1994–95): 5–6 (with Albert Jonsen).

"The Necessary Morality of Foreign Affairs." *Theology Today* 28 (January 1972): 500–503.

"New Mission of an Ancient Faith." *Nexus* 17 (Winter 1974): 8–17.

"Noise the Gathering Crisis." In Paul C. Holmes and Anita J. Lehman, comps., *A Parade of Lines.* San Francisco: Canfield Press, 1971.

"The Nuclear Freeze Resolution." In James P. Sterba, ed., *The Ethics of War and Nuclear Deterrence.* Belmont, CA: Wadsworth, 1985 (with Edward Kennedy).

"Old Growth and the Media: A Lawmaker's Perspective." In Craig L. LaMay and Everette E. Dennis, eds., *Media and the Environment.* Washington, DC: Island Press, 1991.

"The Oregon Connection of Abraham Lincoln . . . February 12, 1984." Springfield, IL: Abraham Lincoln Association, 1985.

"Pastors and Prophets." *Post American* 3 (October 1974): 13–15.

"The Path to Peace." *Theology Today* 26 (January 1970): 390–402.

"The Peace Politics of Mark Hatfield." *Arms Control Today* 17 (April 1987): 32–35.

"Piety and Patriotism." *Post American* 2 (May–June 1973): 1–2.

"Preface," to Thomas Reeves and Karl Hess, *The End of the Draft: A Proposal for Abolishing Conscription and for a Volunteer Army.* New York: Vintage Books, 1970.

"Proclaim Liberty." *Lutheran Standard* 16 (15 June 1976): 4–5.

"Public Policy and Human Engineering." In Craig W. Ellison, ed., *Modifying Man: Implications and Ethics.* Washington, DC: University Press of America, 1978.

Bibliography

"Public Pressure on Higher Education." In G. Kerry Smith, ed., *The Troubled Campus: Current Issues in Higher Education*. San Francisco: Jossey-Bass, 1970.

"Rational Evangelicalism in a Confrontational Age." In Mark O. Hatfield, et al., *The Church Reaches Out: Evangelicalism in the 80s*. Newton Centre, MA: Andover Newton Theological School, 1981.

"Reconciliation and Peace." In Waldo W. Braden, ed., *Representative American Speeches, 1972–1973*. New York: H. W. Wilson, 1973.

"Reflections on a Life of Public Service." In Michael S. Dukakis and Paul Simon, eds., *How to Get into Politics—and Why: A Reader*. Wilmington, MA: Great Source Education Group, 2002.

"Republican Motherhood Redux? Women as Contingent Citizens in 21st Century America." *Journal of Women, Politics and Policy* 29 (2007): 5–30 (with Melody Rose).

"Responding Faithfully as Followers of Jesus Christ in a Nuclear Age." In John A. Bernbaum, ed., *Perspectives on Peacemaking: Biblical Options in the Nuclear Age*. Ventura, CA: Regal Books, 1984.

"Restoring the Balance of Government." *Ripon Forum* 9 (January 1973): 3–5.

"Richard Nixon for President." *Christianity and Crisis* 28 (22 July 1968).

"The Role of the States." *National Civic Review* 48 (December 1959): 562–67.

"Schizophrenia on the Campaign Trail." *Sojourners* 5 (October 1976): 23–25.

"The Shadow of World Hunger." *Moody Monthly* 75 (January 1975): 30–31, 71–73.

"Should the U.S. Constitution Be Amended to Permit School Prayer?" Con—Mark Hatfield. In Steven Anzovin and Janet Podell, eds., *The U.S. Constitution and the Supreme Court*. New York: H. W. Wilson, 1988.

"Should the U.S. Retain Its Present Jurisdiction over the Panama Canal?" *Congressional Digest* 55 (April 1976): 111, 113, 115.

"A Significant Choice." In Richard Halverson, *The Quiet Men: The Secret to Personal Success and Effectiveness by Men Who Practice It*. Los Angeles: Cowman, 1963.

"The Sin That Scarred Our National Soul." *Christian Century* 90 (21 February 1973): 221.

"And Still They Hunger." *Post American* 4 (January 1975): 20–24.

"Stress and the American Worker." *American Psychologist* 45 (1990): 1162–64.

Bibliography

"The Truly Satisfying Life." *American Mercury* 90 (June 1960); reprinted in Merton B. Osborn, comp., *From Darkness to Light: Twenty Testimonies to the Light of the Gospel.* Chicago: Moody Press, 1962.

"U.S. Policy in the Middle East: A Program for Failure?" *American-Arab Affairs* 7 (Winter 1983–84): 17–23.

"Vietnam and American Values." In Ernest W. Lefever, ed., *Ethics and World Politics.* Baltimore: Johns Hopkins University Press, 1972, 74–94.

"Vietnam: A Sobering Postscript." *Post-American* 4 (May 1975): 6–7.

"Vietnam: Charted on a Distorted Map." *Saturday Review* 50 (1 July 1967): 20–22, 28.

"Voice of Dissent: Gov. Hatfield Cites Need for Debate on Viet Nam." Portland *Oregonian,* 6 February 1966, 104.

"War against Disease and Disability." *JAMA* 274, no. 13 (4 October 1995).

"We Kept the 'Obey' in Our Marriage." *Coronet* 48 (June 1960).

"Western and National Water Resources." *AWWA (American Water Works Association)* 57 (1 October 1965): 1231–37.

"What Has Happened to Our Values?" *Eternity* 19 (August 1968): 12–14.

"A World at Stake." *Baptist Student* 47 (May 1968).

"World Hunger: More Explosive Than Atomic Weaponry." *World Vision* 19 (February 1975): 4–8.

"World Hunger—The Religious Connection." *Worldview* 17 (October 1974): 49–53.

HATFIELD UNPUBLISHED SOURCES

Collections Related to Mark O. Hatfield, Archives and Special Collections, Mark O. Hatfield Library, Willamette University, Salem.

Hatfield Collection, Oregon State Archives, Salem.

Mark Hatfield Papers, Archives and Special Collections, Mark O. Hatfield Library, Willamette University, Salem (closed until 2022).

Robert Packwood Papers, Archives and Special Collections, Mark O. Hatfield Library, Willamette University, Salem.

Senator Mark O. Hatfield Oral History Project, Oregon Historical Society, Portland. Includes twenty-four interviews, some of which are with Hatfield's office assistants.

Tom McCall Papers, Oregon Historical Society, Portland.

Travis Cross Papers, Archives and Special Collections, Mark O. Hatfield Library, Willamette University, Salem.

Vertical files, Oregon Historical Society, Portland.

Bibliography

Wayne Morse Papers, University of Oregon Library Special Collections, Eugene.

BOOKS AND ESSAYS ABOUT HATFIELD

"An Inquiry Clears Hatfield." *Time,* 1 October 1984.

Arn, Win. "Rewind: A Conversation with Mark Hatfield." *Covenant Companion,* 7 November 2013; reprint of *Covenant Companion,* 15 August 1972.

AuCoin, Les. *Catch and Release: An Oregon Life in Politics.* Corvallis: Oregon State University Press, 2019.

Balmer, Donald G. "The 1962 Election in Oregon." *Western Political Quarterly* 16 (June 1963): 453–59.

———. "The 1966 Election in Oregon." *Western Political Quarterly* 20 (June 1967): 593–601.

Berke, Richard L. "For Hatfield, a Shining Image Tarnished by Ethics Charges." *New York Times,* 6 June 1991.

Bolduan, Linda M. "The Hatfield Riders: Eliminating the Role of Courts in Environmental Decision Making." *Environmental Law* 20 (1990): 329–85.

Brokaw, Tom. *The Greatest Generation.* New York: Random House, 1998.

Burton, Robert E. *Democrats of Oregon: The Pattern of Minority Politics, 1900–1956.* Eugene: University of Oregon Books, 1970.

Cahn, Robert. "Oregon's Dilemma." *Saturday Evening Post* 234 (14 October 1961): 21–27.

"The Christian and the State." (interview) *Christianity Today* 7 (21 June 1963): 8–11.

Clucas, Richard A., et al., eds. *Oregon Politics and Government: Progressives versus Conservative Populists.* Lincoln: University of Nebraska Press, 2005.

Cornfield, Michael. *Mark O. Hatfield: Republican Senator from Oregon.* Washington, DC: Grossman, 1972.

Cross, Travis. "The 1958 Hatfield Campaign in Oregon." *Western Political Quarterly* 12 (June 1959): 568–71.

Curry, Kevin. "Mark O. Hatfield's Legacy: He Called the Interns." *Hatfield Graduate Journal of Public Affairs* 1 (June 2016): 1–2.

Dement, W. C. "Senator Mark Hatfield: An Advocate for Sleep." *Sleep* 34 (2011): 1443–44.

Drukman, Mason. *Wayne Morse: A Political Biography.* Portland: Oregon Historical Society Press, 1997.

Bibliography

Duscha, Julius. "Mark Hatfield, Man with a Tough Job." *The Reporter* 31 (2 July 1964).

Eells, Robert James. "Mark O. Hatfield and the Search for an Evangelical Politics." PhD. dissertation, University of New Mexico, 1976.

Eells, Robert James, and Bartell Nyberg. *Lonely Walk: The Life of Senator Mark Hatfield.* Chappaqua, NY: Christian Herald Books, 1979.

Egan, Timothy. "Oregon's 'Out-of-Step' Senator Steps Forward." *New York Times,* 26 November 1994.

Etulain, Richard W. *William S. U'Ren: Oregon Father of the Initiative, Referendum, and Recall.* Portland, OR: Chaparral Books, 2020.

Fendall, Lon. *Stand Alone or Come Home: Mark Hatfield as an Evangelical and a Progressive.* Newberg, OR: Barclay Press, 2008.

Fewel, Michael M. "A Rhetorical Analysis of Mark O. Hatfield's Keynote Address to the 1964 Republican National Convention." MA thesis, Washington State University, 1965.

Fitzhenry, James A. "Opinion: The Enduring Legacies of George H. W. Bush and Mark O. Hatfield." *Oregonian,* 3 December 2018.

Friedman, Ralph. "Oregon: Scene of Strange Campaign." *The Progressive* 22 (November 1958): 39–41.

"From Classroom to Capitol: The Academic Politician." *Academe* 81 (May-June 1995).

Goldschmidt, Maure L. "The 1952 Elections in Oregon." *Western Political Quarterly* 6 (March 1953): 123–26.

Granberg, Michaelson, Wesley. "The Peaceable Senator: Mark Hatfield, 1922–2011." *Christian Century,* 24 August 2011.

———. *Unexpected Destinations: An Evangelical Pilgrimage to World Christianity.* Grand Rapids, MI: Wm. B. Eerdmans, 2011.

Hagan, Lowell A. "On Power and Responsibility: A Conversation with Mark Hatfield." *Vanguard* (April 1976).

Halverson, Richard. *The Quiet Men: The Secret to Personal Success and Effectiveness by Men Who Practice It.* Los Angeles: Cowman, 1963.

Hanson, Christopher. "Ethics Issues May Undo Once-Invincible Hatfield." *Seattle Times,* 6 June 1991.

———. "Hatfield Rebuked for Failing to Report Gifts." *Seattle Times,* 13 August 1992.

Henry, Carl F. H. "A Senator's Quandary." *Christianity Today* 17 (18 June 1976).

Johnston, Robert D. "Parties and Politics in Oregon History." *Oregon Historical Quarterly* 110 (Summer 2009): 194–201.

Kirchmeier, Mark. *Packwood: The Public and Private Life from Acclaim to Outrage.* New York: HarperCollins, 1995.

Bibliography

Lafraniere, Sharon, and Bill Mcalister. "Oregon's 'St. Mark'—Hatfield's Career Is Sullied over Conflict of Interest." *Seattle Times,* 31 May 1991.

MacKaye, Milton. "Oregon's Golden Boy." *Saturday Evening Post* 231 (May 1959).

"Mark Hatfield." (interview) *Wittenburg Door* 21 (October–November 1974): 6–13.

"Mark Hatfield Dies: Former Oregon Senator Was 89." (obituary) *Washington Post,* 7 August 2011.

Meet the Press: Sunday, October 25, 1959 with Guests Governor J. Howard Edmondson (Democrat—Oklahoma) and Governor Mark O. Hatfield (Republican—Oregon). St. Paul, MN: 3 MIM Press, 1972.

Meet the Press: Sunday, July 25, 1965 with . . . Mark O. Hatfield (Republican, Oregon) [and five others]. St. Paul, MN: 3 MIM Press, 1972.

Meet the Press: Sunday, January 15, 1967 with . . . Mark O. Hatfield (Republican, Oregon) [and four others]. St. Paul, MN: 3 MIM Press, 1972.

Morecraft, Joseph C., III. "The Counterproductivity of Not Linking Christianity and Politics: A Reply to Senator Mark Hatfield." In Gary North, ed., *The Theology of Christian Resistance: A Symposium.* Tyler, TX: Geneva Divinity School Press, 1983.

Nugent, Walter. *Color Coded: Party Politics in the American West, 1950–2016.* Norman: University of Oklahoma Press, 2018.

"On Power and Responsibility." (interview) *Vanguard* (April 1976): 18–20.

Padrow, Ben. "Mark Hatfield—Oregonian Orator." *Today's Speech* 9 (1961): 11–31.

Peterson del Mar, David. *Oregon's Promise: An Interpretive History.* Corvallis: Oregon State University Press, 2003.

Pippert, Wesley. "Mark O. Hatfield: Prophet or Prodigal?" *Eternity* 22 (May 1971).

Ratcliffe, Ivan W. "Mark Hatfield, a Good Man Speaking Well." Thesis, Southern Illinois University, 1973.

"Relational Religion." (interview) *World Vision* 20 (June 1976): 14–16.

Robbins, William G. *A Man for All Seasons: Monroe Sweetland and the Liberal Paradox.* Corvallis: Oregon State University Press, 2015.

———. *Oregon: This Storied Land.* Seattle: University of Washington Press, [2005] 2020.

Roberts, Arthur O. "Some Relectionsons John Bright and Mark Hatfield." *Quaker Religious Thought* 73 (September 2018): 31–36.

The Scrantons: A Family's Uphill Fight. Chicago: Time, 1964 (includes an article on Mark Hatfield).

Bibliography

"Senator Hatfield Argues That the Draft Is Wrong, a Volunteer Army Is the Answer." *New York Times Magazine,* 30 March 1969, 34–35.

Skillen, James W. "The Purist and the Apologist: A Look at Hatfield's Political Theory." *Reformed Journal* 27 (January 1977).

Swarthout, John M. "The 1956 Election in Oregon." *Western Political Quarterly* 10 (March 1957): 142–50.

———. "The 1958 Election in Oregon." *Western Political Quarterly* 12 (March 1959): 328–44.

Sweeney, Louise. "Senator Mark Hatfield: He Waves a Mean Olive Branch." *Christian Science Monitor,* 17 June 1982.

"Three Members Subject to Investigation by Ethics Committee: George Hansen, Geraldine A. Ferraro, and Sen. Mark Hatfield." *CQ Almanac 1984* (1984): 210–12.

Trumbull, George S. *Governors of Oregon.* Portland: Binfords & Mort, 1959.

"Unexpected Political Hero." *Christianity Today,* 3 October 2011.

Wallis, Jim. "The Courage of Conviction: An Interview with Sen. Mark Hatfield." *Sojourners,* September-October 1996.

Walth, Brent. *Fire at Eden's Gate: Tom McCall and the Oregon Story.* Portland: Oregon Historical Society Press, 1994, 1998.

———. "Hatfield Shifts Gears in Race. " Eugene, OR *Register-Guard,* 21 October 1990.

FILM

The Gentleman of the Senate: Oregon's Mark Hatfield, 2014. Documentary film.

Index

Index

Index

Index

211

Index

CPSIA information can be obtained
at www.ICGtesting.com
Printed in the USA
LVHW030738220821
695820LV00018B/1637

9 780806 175805